Presidents and the Dissolution of the Union

Presidents and the Dissolution of the Union

LEADERSHIP STYLE FROM POLK TO LINCOLN

~

Fred I. Greenstein

With Dale Anderson

PRINCETON UNIVERSITY PRESS

PRINCETON AND OXFORD

Library of Congress Cataloging-in-Publication Data

Greenstein, Fred I., author.
Presidents and the dissolution of the Union : leadership style from Polk
to Lincoln / Fred I. Greenstein with Dale Anderson.
pages cm
Includes bibliographical references and index.
ISBN 978-0-691-15199-1 (hardback)
1. Presidents—United States—History—19th century.   2. Presidents—
United States—Biography.   3. Political leadership—United States—Case
studies.   4. United States—Politics and government—1783–1865.
I. Title.

E176.1.G8294   2013

973.09′9—dc23   2012049032

British Library Cataloging-in-Publication Data is available

This book has been composed in Minion Pro

Printed on acid-free paper. ∞

Printed in the United States of America

1 3 5 7 9 10 8 6 4 2

To James David Barber, Clinton L. Rossiter,
Irving L. Janis, and Richard E. Neustadt

~

They paved the way.

At few other times did policy makers' decisions have such a profound—and calamitous—effect on the nation as they did in the 1840s and 1850s.

—Michael F. Holt, *The Fate of Their Country: Politicians, Slavery Extension, and the Coming of the Civil War*

~ CONTENTS ~

Presidents and the Dissolution of the Union

~ CHAPTER 1 ~

The Presidential Difference in the Civil War Era

> It was not events alone that caused Northerners
> and Southerners to view each other as enemies....
> Politicians ... were largely responsible for the
> ultimate breakdown of the political process.
> —Michael F. Holt, *The Political Crisis
> of the 1850s*[1]

THE MID-NINETEENTH CENTURY witnessed an un-
precedented failure of the American political system.
After two decades of increasingly bitter sectional disagreement, a disastrous war erupted between the
North and the South that took the lives of roughly 2
percent of the nation's population, left much of the
South devastated, and radically remade Southern society. So much has been written on this period, it might
be assumed that no more remains to be said. Nothing
could be further from the truth. The Civil War era is

so intellectually fertile that new ways to explore it constantly arise.

PRESIDENTIAL LEADERSHIP

In the pages that follow, I use the period from 1846 to 1865 as a stage on which a group of American presidents exhibit their strengths and weaknesses. The events of the period from the Mexican-American War to the Civil War form the background of that stage. Six chief executives—James K. Polk, Zachary Taylor, Millard Fillmore, Franklin Pierce, James Buchanan, and Abraham Lincoln—occupy its foreground. These men merit attention because of the demands placed on the chief executive in this momentous era and because they varied so greatly in the caliber of that leadership, ranging from Abraham Lincoln, who ranked first in presidential greatness in a recent poll of historians of the presidency, to James Buchanan, who ranked last.[*2]

This is the third in a series of books that ask what enables some American presidents to meet the challenges of their times and causes others to fail. In *The*

---

[*] C-SPAN conducted the poll of sixty-four historians in 2009. Polk was twelfth, Taylor ranked twenty-ninth; Fillmore was thirty-seventh, Pierce was fortieth, and Buchanan finished forty-second and last. (See http://legacy.c-span.org/PresidentialSurvey/Overall-Ranking.aspx.) Of course, the very notion of "presidential greatness" is problematic because it conflates a president's effectiveness with the merits of his or her policies.

Presidential Difference, I examined the White House occupants from FDR to Barack Obama. In *Inventing the Job of President*, I focused on the seven presidents from George Washington to Andrew Jackson.[3] In all these works, my approach is straightforward. I proceed chronologically, summarizing the formative years, rise to the presidency, and administrations of the protagonists. I then conclude each chapter by assessing the strengths and weaknesses of the president in question by focusing on six realms: public communication, organizational capacity, political skill, policy vision, cognitive style, and emotional intelligence.

Why these qualities? Public communication, using what Theodore Roosevelt called the "bully pulpit," may be thought of as the outer face of the presidency. The ability to articulate goals and rally public support for them is fundamental to presidential leadership. Organization can be viewed as the inner face of the office. The ability to organize and run an administration is vital to a successful presidency. In the smaller administrations of this period, cabinets had much greater significance than they do today. How these presidents filled their cabinets and used those officials and other advisers offers instructive comparisons.

It might be assumed that anyone able to rise to the presidency would be politically skilled, but a surprising number of chief executives has lacked either one or both of two kinds of political skill. Tactical skill is the ability to get results; strategic skill is the ability to get results that stand the test of time. But these skills alone cannot ensure success. Even a consummately skilled president may be an underachiever if he or she lacks a policy vision. At the same time, a president who advances policies that have undesirable consequences is likely to be worse off than one who lacks vision altogether.

A president also needs the appropriate cognitive style to process the torrent of advice and information that comes his or her way. But even the most cerebral of presidents may go astray in the absence of emotional intelligence, the ability to control one's emotions and turn them to advantage rather than succumbing to disabling emotional flaws. That last, as we shall see, is a quality conspicuously lacking in some of the presidents considered in this volume.

The Context of the Times

It remains to fill in the background against which these six presidents performed their duties. In 1845 James K. Polk entered the White House inspired by the example of his mentor Andrew Jackson to be a strong president and with the intention of accomplishing a small number of explicitly defined goals. One of those goals—the acquisition of the Mexican province of

California—led to the Mexican-American War, which produced a far greater territorial growth than he had envisioned. The vast new territory gained by this war, called the Mexican Cession, gave the United States the present-day states of California, Nevada, and Utah; most of Arizona and New Mexico; and parts of Colorado and Wyoming. While a great territorial gain, the Mexican Cession gave rise to an intractable political problem: whether to allow slavery in this area.[4]

Some in the North wanted slavery to be barred from these lands.* Early in the war, Pennsylvania congressman David Wilmot sponsored a measure that would forbid slavery in any territory gained from Mexico. This proposal, the Wilmot Proviso, passed the House of Representatives but not the Senate, but its repeated reintroduction and possible passage was a constant worry to the South until the question was settled in 1850.

The Southern position on the Mexican Cession was staked out in 1847 by John C. Calhoun of South Carolina, who argued that any law prohibiting citizens of any state from entering a territory with their slaves would be "a violation of the Constitution."[5] This stand was the polar opposite of the Wilmot Proviso and, by

---

* Slavery did not exist in the Mexican Cession, as Mexico had abolished slavery, and many politicians North and South insisted that slavery could not exist in most of the area because the soil and climate would not support plantation agriculture. Nevertheless, those politicians became increasingly willing to argue over the principle.

promoting the spread of slavery, marked the extreme in the debate that worried many Northerners.

The political importance of whether states carved from the Mexican Cession would be open to slavery cannot be overstated. At the time, the free states enjoyed a majority of seats in the House, but the North and South had equal representation in the Senate. As a result, the South could block any bills threatening slavery in the Senate. The admission of more free states would overthrow that balance, costing the South this crucial veto power.

When Zachary Taylor became president in 1849, the question of slavery in the Mexican Cession remained unsettled. Later that year, the issue came to a head when California applied for admission as a free state. By that time, many in the South were speaking angrily of secession as the only way to protect their rights. A convention of Southerners held in Nashville in the summer of 1850 asserted the right of states to secede if they saw their rights being threatened and named passage of the Wilmot Proviso as such a threat. This convention also endorsed the idea of extending the Missouri Compromise line* to the Pacific, banning slavery to its north but allowing it to the south, but insisted that only if California was divided in ac-

---

* The Missouri Compromise of 1820 had banned slavery from those parts of the Louisiana Territory, except Missouri, that lay north of the southern border of Missouri, 36°30′ north.

cordance with this line could a free state be admitted into the Union.

In the midst of this crisis, Taylor died in office and was replaced by Vice President Millard Fillmore. The breakup of the Union was temporarily averted by passage of the Compromise of 1850, a package of provisions sponsored initially by Senator Henry Clay of Kentucky that included some measures that advanced the interests of the North and others that appealed to the South. While the compromise did not satisfy the demands of the Nashville Convention, Southern tempers were generally soothed. Across the South—though not in South Carolina—secessionist sentiment waned.

Soon, though, tension reappeared. Many in the North were outraged over the government's enforcement of a key part of the compromise, the Fugitive Slave Act. This act made it far easier than before for Southern agents to seize African Americans from Northern cities under the claim that they were runaway slaves. Many in the North refused to comply with the law, and several Northern states passed personal liberty laws that effectively nullified the Fugitive Slave Act, infuriating Southerners.

Franklin Pierce became president in 1853 in the midst of that bitter controversy. The situation worsened when Congress passed the Kansas-Nebraska Act of 1854, repealing the Missouri Compromise line and authorizing slavery in parts of the Louisiana Territory from which it had hitherto been forbidden. The act sparked widespread anger in the North; six Northern members of Congress denounced the act as

> a gross violation of a sacred pledge; ... a criminal betrayal of precious rights; ... part and parcel of an atrocious plot to exclude from a vast unoccupied region ... free laborers ... and [to] convert it into a dreary region of despotism, inhabited by masters and slaves.[6]

Worse, Kansas quickly erupted in bloodshed as proslavery forces based in Lecompton fought for control of the territory with antislavery forces based in Topeka.

James Buchanan entered the White House in the midst of this fighting. Within days of his 1857 inauguration, the Supreme Court's *Dred Scott* decision mooted the entire debate over slavery in the territories by declaring that Congress had no power to ban the institution from any territory. While Southerners hailed the ruling, many in the North saw the decision as the work of what they called a "Slave Power conspiracy" that threatened the Union. (Chief Justice Roger B. Taney and four of the six justices joining him in the majority opinion were from slave states.)

By the 1860 election, the old Democrat and Whig two-party system had disappeared. The Whig Party had collapsed primarily over the issue of slavery. Many

Northern Whigs moved to an emerging antislavery party, the Republican Party. Some Southern Whigs joined the Democratic Party, giving primacy to their sectional interests, which Democratic policy protected. Other Southern Whigs were at sea, looking for a party that would cool sectional tensions while preserving Southern interests. Many Northern Democrats, meanwhile, had grown frustrated with the increasingly hardline positions of their Southern colleagues.

The Republicans married traditional Whig positions such as support for internal improvements and a protective tariff to a stiff opposition to the spread of slavery to the territories. Support for these policies grew quickly in the North and Midwest but was virtually nonexistent in the South. Southerners regarded the Republicans with suspicion and fear. They believed that the new party intended to abolish slavery, ending their way of life. Soon after Republican Abraham Lincoln won the 1860 presidential election strictly on Northern votes, seven Southern states seceded from the Union and formed the Confederate States of America. The Civil War began little more than a month after Lincoln was inaugurated president.

The Causes of the Civil War

Historians have long debated the causes of the Civil War. Was it an inevitable result of competing social and economic forces, fundamental sectional differences that clashed with the growing pressure to forge a more united nation? Was slavery really the central issue in this conflict, or was it merely "a smoke-screen for concealing the basic motives"?[7] What of the individuals who lived in the Civil War era? What role did they play in the steps that led to the war or the climate that produced it?

As historian Michael Holt points out in the epigraph to this chapter, American political leaders had ample opportunities to work out solutions to the issues they faced in the decade and a half from the Mexican-American War to the Civil War. They could not, however, find a sustaining one. As historian Allan Nevins concludes,

> The angry issue of slavery in the Territories, settled by the great compromise of 1850 but wantonly reopened in 1854, was practically settled again by the end of 1858. But by 1858 passions had been so deeply aroused that large sections of the population could not view the situation calmly or discuss it realistically; fear fed hatred, and hatred fed fear. The unrealities of passion dominated the hour.[8]

Once political leaders reopened that issue, they allowed passion to dominate the hour and did not allow compromise to hold.

What role did the antebellum presidents play in that dynamic? It is important to recognize that the presidency in the 1840s, 1850s, and 1860s was not as powerful an office as it is today, and modern administrations give ample evidence of the limits even on current presidential power. The chief executive of the pre–Civil War era did not control as extensive a federal bureaucracy as in the modern state, and Congress, to some degree, had the initiative as the leading agent in setting federal policy. There is a degree to which, as William J. Andrews explains, presidents in this period "deferred to Congress in most areas."[9]

At the same time, the six presidents of this period were national leaders who wielded executive power and who were expected to provide leadership on major policy issues. Even the four presidents from this period who are generally judged as weak rather than strong executives—Taylor, Fillmore, Pierce, and Buchanan— worked to advance what they saw as the policies best suited to soothe growing sectional animosity. Yet those efforts, as those of congressional compromisers, failed. Presidential leadership in the pre–Civil War era mattered. This book addresses the question of *how* it mattered.

Figure 2.1. James K. Polk's white hair suggests that this photo was taken late in his term; a lithograph from 1845 shows a much younger-looking president. Polk's dedication to work, perhaps inspired by his Calvinist upbringing, prematurely aged him and contributed to his death shortly after leaving the presidency. Source: Library of Congress, LC-USZ62-13011.

~ CHAPTER 2 ~

The Policy-Driven Political Style of James K. Polk

I intend to be, *myself*, president of the United States.

> —James K. Polk, Letter to Cave Johnson, December 21, 1844[1]

Just before his inauguration, Mr. Polk sat in his room with one of those he had selected for one of the departments of the government and speaking energetically, he raised his hand high in the air and bringing it down with force on his thigh said, "there are to be four great measures of my administration: the settlement of the Oregon Question with Great Britain, the acquisition of California [from Mexico] …, the reduction of the tariff to a revenue basis, and the complete and permanent establishment of the Constitutional Treasury.

> —Recollection of George Bancroft, Polk's secretary of the navy, 1866[2]

> The United States will conquer Mexico, but it will
> be as the man who swallows the arsenic, which
> brings him down in turn. Mexico will poison us.
> —Ralph Waldo Emerson,
> Journal, 1846[3]

JAMES K. POLK HAS BEEN CALLED the only strong chief executive between Andrew Jackson and Abraham Lincoln. He also ranks near the top in the perennial polls on greatness in the White House. On the day of his inauguration, Polk declared that his administration would advance "four great measures": division with Great Britain of the jointly administered Oregon Territory, acquisition of California, tariff reduction, and passage of a measure requiring the government to keep its funds in its own vaults instead of in state and private banks.[4] Polk accomplished all this and more in a single four-year term. He also presided over Texas statehood and a victorious war with Mexico. By the time Polk stepped down, more than a million square miles had been added to the nation.

Despite his accomplishments, Polk had a significant failing—he lacked foresight. This was particularly evident in his inability to foresee that his territorial acquisitions would trigger a spiral of controversy that was to come to a head in the Civil War.

Formative Years

James Knox Polk was born near Charlotte, North Carolina, on November 2, 1795. His family moved to central Tennessee when he was a child. Polk's father was Samuel Polk, a prosperous slaveholding planter; his mother was Jane Knox, a devout Presbyterian and distant relative of the sixteenth-century Calvinist theologian John Knox.

During his childhood, Polk was afflicted with many illnesses. The most painful of them was a urological disorder that required an excruciating surgical procedure that was conducted without anesthesia, which was not yet in use. One Polk biographer attributes the intensity of his political leadership to his determination to overcome his suffering and "his mother's unyielding Presbyterianism, with its corollaries of duty, self-reliance, and personal achievement."[5]

Polk's education began under his mother's tutelage, but after recovering from that surgery he was able to attend school near his home. Since the local schools did not provide much in the way of challenge, he took the entrance examination for the University of North Carolina, which he passed with a high score. He was admitted with advanced standing at age twenty and graduated two and a half years later with honors. After college, Polk returned to Tennessee, where he studied law. Although Polk was admitted to the bar, the law was merely his occupation. Politics was his vocation.

Prepresidential Years

Polk forged his political identity in his early years, when he absorbed Jeffersonian republicanism from his family. He solidified it in his twenties when he became a Jacksonian Democrat. Polk's loyalty to Jackson—nicknamed "Old Hickory"—was so strong that he was given the sobriquet "Young Hickory." Like his mentor, Polk favored strong executive power, low tariffs, and economical government.

Polk began his long political career in 1819 by serving as clerk of the Tennessee Senate, a position that provided him with invaluable exposure to the inner workings of politics. Three years later, he was elected to the lower house of the state legislature. Then, in 1825, Polk was elected to his first of seven terms in Congress.

Polk's life took a significant turn in 1824 when he married the politically astute Sarah Childress. Polk's wife was to become a major influence on his political career. As her biographer puts it, she "was not just a politician's wife whose sole interest was entertaining." Instead, she had a thorough grasp on politics and

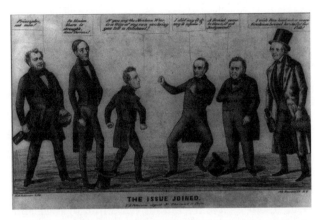

Figure 2.2. A pugnacious President Polk (*left center*) prepares to square off against Whig senator Daniel Webster in an 1846 political cartoon. Like many Whigs, Webster had denounced the Mexican-American War as unjustified. In the cartoon, Polk objects, "If you say the Mexican War is a War of my own makeing you tell a falshood! [*original spelling*]" Webster responds, "I did say it & say it again!" The two fighters are backed by journalists who endorsed their respective positions, including (*far right*) *New York Tribune* editor Horace Greeley, perhaps the nation's premier journalist from the 1840s until his death in 1872. Source: Library of Congress, LC-USZ62-21790.

policy and gave her husband political advice. Beyond that, Sarah Polk's gracious and affable manner helped balance her husband's cold, unbending demeanor.[6]

The next politically important event in Polk's career was the 1828 presidential election, in which Andrew Jackson swept President John Quincy Adams out of office with 56 percent of the popular vote and 78 percent of the electoral vote. Polk became Jackson's chief lieutenant in the House, first as chairman of the Ways and Means Committee and then in the even more powerful office of Speaker. In that post, he played an invaluable part in Jackson's conflict with the Whigs and his victorious war with the Bank of the United States.

In 1839 Polk was prevailed upon to run for governor of Tennessee on the grounds that he had the best chance to carry the state for the Democrats. Polk was elected, but he lost his bid for reelection in 1841 and an effort to regain the office in 1843. These defeats led many politicians to conclude that Polk's political career was over. But when the Democrats convened in Baltimore in May of 1844 for that year's presidential nominating convention, his allies proposed him as the running mate of former president Martin Van Buren, who was seeking to return to the White House.

It had been widely assumed that Van Buren would be the nominee, but he alienated the still-influential Jackson by opposing the annexation of Texas. Jackson then threw his support to Polk, who favored annexation. After Van Buren failed to win the required two-thirds of the delegates, the convention nominated Polk on the ninth ballot.

Polk's opponent in the general election was the Whig Party founder and perennial presidential candidate Henry Clay.* Polk was the victor by 170 to 105 votes in the electoral college despite having only a razor-thin popular margin. A shift of little more than 5,000 of the 485,000 votes cast in New York State would have made Clay the winner.[7] Polk, not yet fifty years old, became the youngest man to date elected president.

A Policy-Driven President

Polk's policy-driven leadership was evident in his inaugural address, in which he declared that "ours was meant to be a plain and frugal government" and presented a "concise enumeration" of his policy goals, which included the four major objectives detailed by George Bancroft in one of the chapter's epigraphs.[8] By the summer of Polk's second year in office, three of these goals had been achieved: a law that reduced tariffs and made them nonprotective, creation of a government treasury, and division of the Oregon Territory with Great Britain.

Polk's hands-on leadership style was central to these achievements. When, for example, he learned

---

* The voters also had a chance to opt for a tiny antislavery party that proved to be important in the election's outcome. Liberty Party candidate James G. Birney took enough New York votes from Clay to cost him the state and the election.

that the Ways and Means Committee had inserted protectionist provisions in his tariff bill, he button-holed its chairman and persuaded him to remove them. Similarly, when he learned that a senator whose vote was crucial for passage of that tariff was leaving the capital on a personal errand, Polk arranged for him to be intercepted at the train station and ushered to the White House, where he persuaded the law-maker to remain and cast his vote.[9]

Polk's negotiations with Great Britain over the division of the Oregon Territory illustrate his shrewd bargaining style. Polk initially proposed that the boundary between American and British Oregon be drawn at the present-day border between Canada and the United States. When Britain refused this proposal, he upped the ante and took the position of those Americans who favored a more northern boundary that would give the United States present-day British Columbia. Britain then relented and accepted Polk's original proposal. The agreement gave the United States undisputed control over the vast area now encompassed by Oregon, Washington, Idaho, and portions of Montana and Wyoming.

Polk's remaining goal was to gain possession of California. He first tried to purchase the area from Mexico, but that nation—angry over the American annexation of Texas in 1845—refused to meet his emissary. Thus thwarted, Polk turned to provoking a war. He ordered General Zachary Taylor to move American troops into an area claimed by both Mexico and the United States. Before long, a Mexican force ambushed some of those troops. Polk then informed Congress that Mexico had "shed American blood upon the American soil" and urged the lawmakers to acknowledge that a state of war existed between the two nations, which they promptly did.

The war with Mexico was barely underway when there was a significant and ominous development. Congressman David Wilmot of Pennsylvania introduced an amendment to an appropriations bill that would bar slavery from any territory acquired from Mexico. As explained in chapter 1, the Wilmot Proviso contributed to the sectional polarization in Congress and was part of the chain of causality that ended with the Civil War.

WAGING WAR WITH MEXICO

Polk was unstinting in his leadership in the war with Mexico. The range of his efforts has been summarized by Leonard White:

> He determined the general strategy of military and naval operations; he chose commanding officers; he

gave personal attention to supply problems; he ener-
gized so far as he could the General Staff; he controlled the military and naval estimates; and he used
the cabinet as a major coordinating agency for the
conduct of the campaign.[10]

The United States prevailed in every major battle
of the war, in part because of the able generalship of
commanders Zachary Taylor and Winfield Scott. Taylor invaded Mexico by land from the north; Scott led
an amphibious invasion that captured Veracruz on
the Gulf of Mexico. Scott's forces fought their way to
Mexico City, which fell in September 1847. American
forces also secured control of California and New
Mexico. The war ended in February 1848 with the
signing of the Treaty of Guadalupe Hidalgo, which resulted in the Mexican Cession.

The war with Mexico was the object of bitter debate, both in itself and because of the issue of the
spread of slavery. When the Wilmot Proviso was introduced, Polk described it as "foolish and mischie-
vous," adding that he found it "difficult to conceive"
that there was a connection between "slavery and
making peace with Mexico."[11] Though he believed in
American expansion, Polk had no interest in spread-
ing slavery. Indeed, he thought that the Missouri Compromise line should be extended into the Mexican
Cession and that, though slavery would be allowed in

the "narrow ribbon of territory south of" that line, it "would probably never exist" there.[12] It appears not to have occurred to him that contention over the status of slavery in the Mexican Cession was bound to occur. This failure provides an example of his political shortsightedness.

LEADERSHIP QUALITIES

Public Communication

Polk placed a premium on communicating his policies to the public when he campaigned in Tennessee. He was so effective that he was known as the "Napoleon of the stump." Once in the White House, Polk followed the contemporary practice of advancing presidential policies in an administration newspaper. In another example of his hands-on presidential style, he met regularly with the paper's editor to establish how it would present his administration's policies. He was adamant about having his own man in this role; when Andrew Jackson took issue with him for abandoning the existing Democratic newspaper, Polk refused to give in. To ensure that the paper's message reflected his thinking, Polk occasionally wrote editorials himself or instructed cabinet members to do so.

Organizational Capacity

Polk was distinctive for the extent to which he dominated his administration. Not only did he set its overall policies, but he also managed its most minute
details. He made up for the failure of Congress to
appropriate funds for presidential aides by making
extensive use of his wife and employing his nephew
as his private secretary. Polk also used the members
of his cabinet as the equivalent of the modern West
Wing, particularly in legislative liaison work; for example, when the House of Representatives was voting
on Polk's proposal to reduce the price of public land,
five of the six cabinet members were in the chamber
corralling votes.[13]

Political Skill

Polk excelled in employing what political scientist
Robert A. Dahl refers to as "slack resources," that is,
unrecognized potential sources of political power.[14]
He was better at advancing his policies than at anticipating their effects, however. As historian Sam W.
Haynes puts it, Polk focused "intently on objects close
at hand" but failed to identify problems "that lay on
the distant horizon."[15] It is also worth noting that
Polk's controversial war with Mexico contributed to
the Democrats losing their majority in the House of

Representatives in 1846 and the White House in 1848. Polk's leadership style illustrates the difference between tactical and strategic political skill—that is, the ability to get results in the short run versus the ability to anticipate the consequences of one's actions.

Policy Vision

The four-point agenda that Polk enunciated on his inauguration day was not his own invention. As a stout Jacksonian, he joined other Democrats in favoring low tariffs, low governmental expenditures, and westward expansion and opposing such "internal improvements" as the construction of turnpikes and canals. Historian David M. Pletcher argues that "much of Polk's foreign policy was improvised from month to month in response to events."[16] Ad hoc policy making may indicate political nimbleness, but it does not suggest vision.

Cognitive Style

Polk's mind was incisive but narrow. His interests began and ended with politics, as can be seen from his four-volume diary, which is virtually devoid of references to literature and the fine arts. He put heroic effort into mastering the specifics of his presidency, sometimes exceeding his cabinet secretaries in his mastery of the workings of their departments. In the final months of his presidency, he noted in his diary that he had not convened his cabinet for over a month, adding:

> I have conducted the government without their aid. I have become so familiar with the duties and workings of the government, not only upon general principles, but in most of its minute details, that I had but little difficulty in doing this. I have made myself acquainted with the duties of the subordinate officers, and have probably paid more attention to details than any of my predecessors.[17]

Emotional Intelligence

Polk spent long hours at his job, working to the point of exhaustion. If asked to assess his personality, a modern clinician might conclude that Polk tended toward an obsessive-compulsive personality disorder. In contrast to most public officials of his time, he remained in the capital during the steamy summer months, leaving the city for only six weeks during the four years of his presidency. Washington journalist Ben Perley Poore later noted that even midway through his term "his friends were pained to witness his shortened and enfeebled step, and the air of languor and exhaustion which sat upon him."[18] Polk's efforts took an inevitable toll. He looked haggard by the time his term ended and died less than four months after leaving office after contracting an illness in a post-presidency tour of the South.[19] But Polk's lack of emotional intelligence presents a paradox—it accounts not only for his failures but also for his successes.

Figure 3.1. Zachary Taylor, photographed in 1849, had a reputation for a fiery temper and prickly personality that seems belied by the firm but grandfatherly expression shown here. The career soldier also looks less stiff and more comfortable being photographed than many of his contemporaries. Source: Library of Congress, LC-USZ62-8209.

~ CHAPTER 3 ~

The Rough and Ready Leadership of Zachary Taylor

Few presidents ever needed an effective spokesman in Congress as acutely as did Taylor; none ever lacked such a spokesman more conspicuously.
—David M. Potter, *The Impending Crisis: 1848–1861*[1]

The people of the North need have no apprehension of the further extension of slavery.
—Zachary Taylor, speech at Mercer, Pennsylvania, August 1849[2]

For more than a half a century ..., this Union has stood unshaken.... In my judgment its dissolution would be the greatest of calamities ... I shall stand by it and maintain its integrity to the full extent of the obligations imposed and the powers conferred upon me by the Constitution.
—Zachary Taylor, Message to Congress, December 4, 1849[3]

ZACHARY TAYLOR WAS an accomplished career officer who lived up to the nickname "Old Rough and Ready." Having risen through the ranks of the U.S. Army to general, Taylor achieved his greatest success in the Mexican-American War, which propelled him to the nation's highest office. It comes as no surprise that Taylor governed the nation in a manner better suited for the battlefield than the White House.[4]

GROWING UP A SOLDIER

Taylor was born on September 24, 1784, in Orange County, Virginia, to Richard Taylor, a prominent Virginia planter and Revolutionary War officer, and the former Sarah Dabney Strother. Growing up on the frontier, young Taylor had a spotty education. From an early age, though, he aspired to be a soldier, and in May 1808, he was commissioned as a first lieutenant in the Seventh Infantry. Two years later, Taylor married Margaret Mackall Smith. Early in 1812, Taylor was promoted to captain and sent to the Indiana Territory to take command of Fort Knox, which the commander had fled. In a few weeks, he restored the garrison to order.

Later that year, after being reassigned, Taylor earned public acclaim for his successful defense of a strategically located fort against an Indian war party. He was promoted to major but was reduced to captain at the end of the War of 1812 and, in a fit of anger, left the army in 1815. He returned to the service the following year at his desired rank and spent the next three decades in various frontier posts. In 1832 Taylor commanded all regular troops in the Black Hawk War, but he did not take part in any major battles. In the Second Seminole War, by contrast, Taylor led his troops to a significant victory in the Battle of Lake Okeechobee. In recognition, he was promoted to brigadier general.

In April 1845 President Polk directed Taylor to establish a base in Texas to defend the newly annexed state against any Mexican attack. Taylor made his base near Corpus Christi on the Nueces River and trained an army of volunteers. In March 1846, following Polk's further orders, Taylor moved his troops into territory adjacent to the Rio Grande. Mexico had never accepted the American claim for the territory between the Nueces and the Rio Grande, and on April 26, 1846, a Mexican force ambushed a party of Americans, killing eleven and capturing dozens. This fight led to the congressional declaration or war.

By February 1847, Taylor had won a series of battles at Palo Alto, Resaca de la Palma, Monterrey, and Buena Vista. The last victory, in which Taylor's forces won despite being outnumbered three to one, earned the general instant fame. His refusal to surrender despite those long odds, his stubbornly holding ground rather than retreating at a crisis point, and his remaining in the center of the fight atop his beloved horse, "Old Whitey," added to Taylor's luster.

Ascent to the Presidency

On December 2, 1847, Taylor returned to the United States and began his transition from soldier to would-be politician. Leaders of both parties recognized that the overwhelmingly popular Taylor would make an ideal presidential candidate. They were drawn to him not only because of this popularity but also because he had avoided taking a stand on the issues of the day. Taylor had a significant shortcoming, however; no one knew which party he favored.

Before long, Taylor resolved some of the mystery by declaring that he was "a Whig but not an ultra [extreme] Whig." Taylor acknowledged that as a career soldier he did not know the "minute details of political legislation";[5] in fact, he had never even voted because he believed that, as a professional soldier, he should be above politics. Despite this lack of political experience, he made it known that he was available for the presidency. Many Whig leaders argued that Taylor's ambiguity made him an ideal candidate, but

THE CANDIDATE OF MANY PARTIES.
A Phrenological Examination to Ascertain what His Political Principles Are.

Figure 3.2. Under the observant eye of Whig journalist Horace Greeley, a phrenologist examines the skull of candidate Zachary Taylor during the 1848 election year to determine his political principles and temperament. Phrenology was a nineteenth-century pseudo-science that claimed to determine intelligence and character from the bumps on an individual's head. The cartoonist gives Taylor high ratings in combativeness and firmness, in which he is labeled so "obstinate" as to be "mulish." Source: Library of Congress, LC-USZ62-19668.

others questioned his qualifications. As one dissenter put it, the old soldier's strengths consisted only of "sleeping forty years in the woods and cultivating moss on the calves of his legs."[6]

Despite these doubters, the 1848 Whig nominating convention took only one day to name Taylor to oppose the Democrats' Lewis Cass. In the months following the convention, Taylor kept a low profile by campaigning through surrogates. Taylor's backers were deliberately ambiguous—in the South, they left the impression that, as a slaveholder, he could be counted on to back the expansion of slavery; in the North, they implied that he was prepared to sign the Wilmot Proviso, thus barring slavery from the Mexican Cession.

Taylor amassed 163 electoral votes to 127 for Cass. As in the 1844 election, antislavery votes in New York State decided the outcome. Former president Martin Van Buren, the Free-Soil party candidate, won more than 120,000 votes in his native New York. Those votes gave Taylor, rather than Cass, the state's 36 electoral votes—precisely his margin of victory.

A Truncated Presidency

While he ran as a Whig, Taylor saw himself as a president above party. Before the election, he declared in a public letter his desire to "be untrammeled [and] unpledged, so as to be president of the nation [and] not of a party."[7] He even vowed to distribute patronage jobs proportionately among Whigs, Democrats, and members of the Native American party, a nativist, or anti-immigration, party then taking shape. If Taylor had any political agenda, it was to put an end to partisanship and rising sectional divisions. A lifelong soldier, he was, above all, a nationalist.

Taylor was hampered in naming his cabinet by his lack of contact with Whig politicians and by poor relations and policy disagreements with Whig icons Henry Clay and Daniel Webster. Seeking a regionally balanced cabinet, he named three members from the North and Old Northwest, two from border states, and two from the South. Four of his choices were noted lawyers of the time, though the group had little experience on Capitol Hill, which might have hurt Taylor's ability to work with Congress. Most tellingly, none of his choices were allied with the "ultra Whigs" Clay and Webster, as Taylor moved to elevate his own backers in an effort to recast the party as a more moderate organization.

Despite his seeming political innocence, Taylor had the sagacity to follow a clear and determined course to break up the congressional logjam over the organization of Mexican Cession lands. Shortly after taking office, he dispatched Georgia congressman Thomas Butler King to California, instructing him to urge California to bypass the territorial period and apply directly for statehood. Taylor's aim was to circumvent the contention that would follow if California entered the Union as a territory, which would leave Congress to decide whether it would be a slave or free state.

On December 4, 1849, Taylor delivered what would be his only annual message to Congress, informing the lawmakers that he expected California to apply for statehood soon and New Mexico to follow before long. He also declared that he did not view it as consistent with the Constitution for the president to veto legislation unless he deemed it to be unconstitutional. This statement alarmed slaveholders, who feared it meant Taylor would sign the Wilmot Proviso.

Taylor's message reached a Congress even more bitterly divided than it had been during Polk's administration. When Congress convened in December, the House needed fifty-nine ballots and nearly three weeks to elect a Speaker. Worse for Taylor, Southerners in Congress had grown more alarmed about their ability to maintain equality in the Senate. The president's plan increased their anxiety. Georgia's Robert Toombs—a fellow Whig—stated the Southern fear in a fiery speech:

> If, by your legislation, you seek to drive us from the territories of California and New Mexico, purchased by the common blood and treasure of the whole people,... thereby attempting to fix a national degradation upon half the states of this Confederacy, I am for disunion.[8]

Toombs's position underscores how the political climate had shifted. In February 1849 he had supported the idea of immediate California statehood, even though it would be a free state. It was in this context that Southern states called for a convention, which would meet in Nashville in June 1850, in an effort to find a united Southern voice. Southerners in Congress also tried to appeal directly to the president in February 1850. In a meeting with some of them, Taylor made it clear that he would brook no talk of secession. He bluntly told them that if any state seceded, he would call out the army and lead it himself, adding that anyone "taken in rebellion against the Union, he would hang ... with less reluctance than he had hanged deserters and spies in Mexico."[9]

For the first half of 1850, Congress was engaged in a historic debate over this and related issues. The topic was a series of resolutions proposed by Henry Clay in January 1850 that addressed the interests of both the North and the South. Clay was convinced that Taylor's proposal would never pass Congress. Taylor remained committed to his own plan of promoting admission of both California and New Mexico as free states, which appealed only to the North. Clay's proposal prompted debate in Congress that lasted months. It was widely assumed that Taylor would have vetoed Clay's more politically feasible plan, but on July 9 the president died. His death produced a profound policy shift, as successor Millard Fillmore supported the Clay compromise. As Michael Holt observes, "No event was more important in securing passage of the Compromise of 1850."[10] How that passage was achieved is explored in the following chapter.

Leadership Qualities

Public Communication

Taylor's public communications were a mixed bag. On the one hand, no one had reason to be confused about his views on the extension of slavery into the Mexican Cession. On the other hand, the nuggets of information in his artless public communications were few and far between. Historian David Potter dismisses Taylor's communication, judging that he "could not articulate [his views] well, being politically naïve and unskillful with words."[11]

Taylor was also handicapped, in Potter's judgment, by the lack of a strong voice in Congress in favor of his views. The senator with whom he developed the closest relationship was New York's William Seward. Seward helped doom Taylor's California and New Mexico policy, however, in his speech on Clay's compromise plan. He framed blocking the expansion of slavery as a moral issue, citing the need to follow a "higher law" than the Constitution. This stance angered Southerners and forced Taylor to issue a quick and emphatic rebuke in the administration newspaper.

As the Seward episode shows, for all his seeming lack of political sophistication, Taylor was aware of the importance of a presidentially sponsored newspaper in advancing his program. Indeed, even before arriving in Washington, he had accepted the offer of an experienced journalist to edit his administration's mouthpiece. Of course, Taylor's ability to make full use of that editor was largely untested because of the brevity of his presidency.

Organizational Capacity

Taylor was largely a hands-off president. As a career soldier, he was devoted to the chain of command. As a result, he delegated considerable authority to his cabinet officers and also left patronage decisions largely up to them. Yet the men he appointed can be best described as "solid" and "generally respectable";[12] they were hardly standout figures. Historians have criticized him for not including supporters of Clay and Webster, but historian Elbert Smith argues that this choice reflects Taylor's hope to redefine the Whigs in a less extreme direction.

Political Skill

Taylor was described by contemporaries as "a man of strong and blind prejudices" and a man who was "easily … thrown off his balance by trifles."[13] Biographer

K. Jack Bauer says that he was viewed as having a massive temper when it exploded, and he was certainly a neophyte to politics. All of this is consistent with his unbending insistence on advancing his own plan for addressing the status of slavery in the Mexican Cession. He showed some shrewdness in trying to bypass congressional debate over territorial status and jumping directly to statehood for California and New Mexico, but his plan was politically doomed by the fact that Southern legislators would not accept being thus outflanked.

As Taylor had spent his life outside politics, he did not have the political connections, or abilities, to turn that plan into a reality. Unfortunately, the times called for a president with consummate political skill. In Bauer's judgment, one of Taylor's weaknesses was that he could not advance his policies by using members of his cabinet, given their "limited influence in Congress."[14] He goes on to say, "At no place does Taylor's lack of political experience show more clearly than in his failure to recognize the necessity of creating a substantial bloc of congressional supporters."[15]

Policy Vision

Preservation of the Union was Taylor's overriding political principle. Though a Southerner, his loyalty to the nation transcended his attachment to his region.

This accounts for Taylor's opposition to policies he considered divisive and his readiness to use force against secessionists. Given the shortness of his term and the significance of the slavery issue, his views on other issues played little role in his presidency.

Cognitive Style

"Zachary Taylor," Bauer writes, "was not an intellectual and demonstrated only limited curiosity about the world around him, except for agricultural developments. Even there, he expressed little interest about aspects which did not appear to have some value to his plantations."[16] Taylor had only a rudimentary education. Rival general Winfield Scott remarked that Taylor's "mind had not been enlarged and refreshed by reading, or much converse with the world."[17]

Emotional Intelligence

As Bauer points out, the paucity of sources on Taylor's early years makes it difficult to assess his emotional intelligence. His taciturn demeanor contributed further to the difficulty of plumbing his psyche. Still, Taylor had a number of attributes that do much to account for his failure to compromise, such as his lack of self-control, "his strong and blind prejudices," and his explosive temper. None of this speaks well for his emotional intelligence.

Figure 4.1. Millard Fillmore looks dignified in this portrait apparently taken after his brief stint in the presidency. Fillmore's face suggests the modest satisfaction he expressed in his final message to Congress, in which he claimed to have filled the office "to the best of my humble ability, [and] with a single eye to the public good" and stated his "devout gratitude" that he "[left] the country in a state of peace and prosperity" (Smith, *Presidencies of Taylor & Fillmore*, 249). Source: Library of Congress, LC-DIG-cwpbh -00697.

CHAPTER 4

Millard Fillmore and the Compromise of 1850

[Fillmore] overcame the disadvantages of desperate childhood poverty to become an outstanding state official and U.S. Representative and a responsible and highly effective President during a time of great national crisis.

> —Elbert B. Smith, "Millard Fillmore"
> in Leonard W. Levy and
> Louis Fisher, eds., *Encyclopedia
> of the American Presidency*[1]

If the laws of the United States are opposed or obstructed in any State or Territory by combinations too powerful to be suppressed by the judicial or civil authorities,... it is the duty of the President either to call out the militia or to employ the military and naval force of the United States or to do both if in his judgment the exigency of the occasion shall so require.

> —Millard Fillmore, Special Message
> to Congress, August 6, 1850[2]

> It was hardly to have been expected that the series
> of measures passed at your last session with the
> view of healing the sectional differences which had
> sprung from the slavery and territorial questions
> should at once have realized their beneficent
> purpose.... I believe they were necessary to allay
> asperities and animosities that were rapidly
> alienating one section of the country from another.
> —Millard Fillmore, First Annual
> Message to Congress,
> December 2, 1850[3]

ZACHARY TAYLOR DIED on July 9, 1850, and Vice
President Millard Fillmore unexpectedly became the
thirteenth president of the United States. Fillmore had
been sidelined in his predecessor's administration,
but in his capacity as presiding officer of the Senate,
he had carefully followed the heated congressional debate over the status of slavery in the Mexican Cession.
Plunged immediately into a crisis when he assumed
the presidency, Fillmore played a critical part in the
enactment of compromise legislation that appeared at
the time to have averted the threat of a war between
the slave and free states.[4]

EARLY YEARS AND POLITICAL RISE

Millard Fillmore was the personification of the American success story, a self-made man. He was born into

deep poverty on January 7, 1800, to Nathaniel Fillmore, a farmer in central New York State, and the former Phoebe Millard. With but sporadic schooling, Millard Fillmore could barely read even into his late teens, but he improved his skill by reading anything he could and looking up unfamiliar words in a dictionary he kept with him at all times. Like fellow Whig Abraham Lincoln, Fillmore took his dedication to self-improvement beyond voracious reading. He took classes in a local school when he could and later managed to master the law, pass the bar, and rise to become a prosperous attorney. Shortly after beginning his legal career, he married Abigail Powers, two years his senior, who had briefly been his teacher when he was a young man.

Fillmore embarked on his political career in 1828 by winning a seat in the New York state legislature, to which he was reelected. In 1832 he was elected to the first of four terms in the U.S. House of Representatives. During that time, Fillmore was the author of the tariff of 1842, chaired the powerful Ways and Means Committee, and was the runner-up in the 1841 election for Speaker of the House.

By the time Fillmore left the House of Representatives, he had become a respected and influential member of Congress. But the Fillmores disliked living in Washington, and they returned to New York State in 1843. After losing a race as governor, he served as state comptroller, where he sketched out the principles of new state banking laws and created a new system for backing the state currency that served as a model for the system adopted by Congress during the Civil War. At that point, Fillmore might well have contented himself with spending the rest of his life in his home state, but he was chosen by the Whig Party as Zachary Taylor's 1848 running mate to provide regional balance to the ticket headed by a Southerner.

Fillmore played a marginal role in the Taylor administration. While most nineteenth-century vice presidents were marginalized, Fillmore's situation was particularly galling. Taylor leaned for advice on New York's William Seward, who came from the eastern, more liberal faction of the state party that the conservative westerner Fillmore opposed. Fillmore complained bitterly about being ignored regarding not only policy but also patronage: "My recommendations in my own State and even in my own city have been disregarded. My advice has neither been sought nor given as to the policy to be pursued."[5] The vice president was even unable to win patronage jobs for his law partner and for the son of a close friends. He was also treated with disdain by Taylor's cabinet.

Then, on July 4, 1850, Taylor was stricken by an acute attack of gastroenteritis and five days later died in what the historian David M. Potter has described as "one of those extraneous events which suddenly and in an irrational way alter the course of history."[6]

An Accidental President

The shift from Taylor to Fillmore was consequential because Fillmore differed from his predecessor on the question of how the nation should resolve the issue of the status of slavery in the Mexican Cession. Taylor had proposed that California and New Mexico be admitted to the Union as free states, a plan that appealed only to the North. Fillmore, on the other hand, had come to favor the more comprehensive plan sponsored by Kentucky senator Henry Clay, which had provisions appealing to both North and South.

Clay's compromise consisted of admission of California to the Union as a free state, abolition of the sale of slaves in the District of Columbia, and passage of a draconian fugitive slave act that provided a greater financial incentive for returning African Americans to their alleged masters than for setting them free.[7] There was also provision for Texas to give up land it claimed in New Mexico in return for a $10 million payment and for organization of New Mexico and Utah as territories. A Democratic amendment was approved that would allow or ban slavery from New Mexico or Utah according to the wishes of the territories' residents.

That amendment introduced the principle of "popular sovereignty," which eventually became the grounds on which those territories were organized.

After initially supporting Taylor's idea, Fillmore had concluded by late June that he would vote in favor of Clay's compromise if the Senate vote came to a tie. His determination to support Clay's plan was buttressed when he took office and was given a letter sent to Taylor by Texas governor Peter Bell, who threatened to send the Texas militia to take possession of the New Mexico land his state claimed. Alarmed, Fillmore sent 750 additional federal troops to Santa Fe and dispatched a warning to Bell.

Soon after taking office, Fillmore also accepted the pro forma resignations of members of Taylor's cabinet and replaced them with supporters of Clay's bill, including the Whig giant Daniel Webster. Most historians have viewed this as evidence of Fillmore's decisiveness, but historian Paul Finkelman has asserted the questionable view that the decision left him shorthanded at a time when he most needed aides.[8] Given Webster's contribution to the eventual passage of the Compromise of 1850, Fillmore hardly seems to have been without resources. In addition, given his treatment by the men in Taylor's cabinet, it is unlikely that Fillmore could have worked effectively with them.

Before Fillmore completed his first month in office, however, the compromise bill seemed doomed.

In July, after weeks of rancorous debate and countless amendments had been proposed and discussed, Clay's comprehensive bill failed to pass either house. Democratic senator Stephen A. Douglas remained dedicated to having the compromise enacted, however. Convinced that the strategy of putting all the measures in one giant bill was flawed by making it easy for opponents of both pro-North and pro-South features to vote it down, he split the measure into five separate bills.

Fillmore himself was indispensable to the passage of Douglas's five-part Compromise of 1850.[9] First, he sent a message to Congress revealing Governor Bell's threat, stating his own resolve to use force against Texas if necessary, and urging Congress to enact a law settling the boundary. Then, when the bills came to a vote, he pressured Northern Whigs to abstain from voting on the fugitive slave bill and the one organizing territorial governments in New Mexico and Utah without settling the slavery question, both of which many Northern Whigs opposed. Their abstentions allowed both bills to pass, and their votes in favor of the pro-North bills—also encouraged by Fillmore—ensured passage of those measures. The president signed each bill into law as Congress approved it, the last signing coming on September 20, little more than two months after he had taken office. At the end, Fillmore expressed relief that "the long agony is over."[10]

Fillmore hailed the compromise as an action that would calm the growing sectional ferment. The new Fugitive Slave Act doomed national harmony, however. Southerners placed great emphasis on this law. A secession convention was held in Georgia soon after the compromise was passed.* While the delegates voted down secession in overwhelming numbers, they issued a stark warning in a statement of principles called the Georgia Platform: "Upon the faithful execution of the *Fugitive Slave [Act]* by the proper authorities depends the preservation of our much beloved Union."[11]

Under such pressure, the Fillmore administration took steps to enforce the act, going so far as to try a trio of Pennsylvania Quakers for treason for helping fugitives avoid seizure and escape to Canada. Northerners, outraged by the seizure of people who had lived in the North for years, began to obstruct the law. This conflict lost Fillmore support across the North and helped fracture the Whig Party. Elbert Smith writes that Fillmore supported the law only reluctantly, after "a painful inner struggle in which he decided that the salvation of the Union and the prevention of a civil war were goals that transcended his conscience on the immediate slavery questions."[12] Nevertheless, enforce it he did.

---

*Conventions were considered in three other states as well, but they never materialized, in part because leaders in those states agreed with the Georgia stand.

Figure 4.2. This engraving, titled *Union* and celebrating the Compromise of 1850, is emblematic of Millard Fillmore's unassuming personality and the general disregard for his contribution. He is relegated to the far right corner, towered over by the members of Congress arrayed behind and beside him. Rather than honoring the president, the work celebrates the three legislative giants who dominated the 1820s to 1850: Henry Clay (*seated in the center*), who authored the compromise but could not get it passed; South Carolina's John C. Calhoun (*to his right*), who denounced the compromise in the last speech he gave before dying; and Daniel Webster (*to the right of the bust of George Washington*), Fillmore's secretary of state and a procompromise ally. Source: Library of Congress, LC-USZ62-14031.

At the same time, Fillmore was evenhanded in his actions. While enforcement of the Fugitive Slave Act angered northerners, he also took steps that thwarted goals Southerners cherished. Adhering to neutrality laws, Fillmore moved to block efforts by proslavery adventurers—called "filibusterers"— to seize territory in Central America, which they hoped to then join to the United States through annexation. As that result would have increased the number of slave states, the filibusterers' efforts were widely supported in the South.

Fillmore's evenhandedness was politically costly. As he lamented later, "In the North I was charged with being a pro-slavery man, seeking to extend slavery over free territory, and in the South I was accused of being an abolitionist. But I am neither."[13] In 1852 he sought his party's nomination for the presidency in his own right. Northern Whigs overwhelmingly backed Mexican-American War hero General Winfield Scott, and Fillmore lost the nomination to him. Four years later, Fillmore finished third in the presidential race as the candidate of the nativist Know-Nothing party—though he rejected its anti-immigrant stand and ran as a Unionist. He then retired from public life, re-emerging when the Civil War broke out to encourage volunteers and support the Union cause.

LEADERSHIP QUALITIES

Public Communication

Communication with the public played only a modest part in the Fillmore presidency. Like other Whigs, Fillmore did not make extensive use of newspapers as tools of presidential communication. Nevertheless, he did recognize that such a device could sometimes be advantageous and, after taking office, he replaced Taylor's presidential newspaper with one of his own choosing. Fillmore's public messages to Congress were detailed and closely argued. They could degenerate at times into the kind of stiff, obscure language, exemplified by the last epigraph to this chapter, but he could be also effectively direct, as when stating his intention to oppose any use of force by Texas in New Mexico in the second epigraph.

Organizational Capacity

Fillmore showed his attentiveness to organization at the outset of his presidency by replacing Taylor's cabinet with Whigs who favored Henry Clay's proposed compromise. They included political giant Daniel Webster, who was helpful in pressuring members of Congress to follow administration wishes. Fillmore also showed good judgment in his handling of patronage jobs. Resisting pressure to replace all Taylor's appointees, he allowed those he viewed as able to remain in office. Nevertheless, he did make an effort to reward longtime loyal Whigs who had been eclipsed by Taylor's patronage decisions.

Political Skill

Fillmore was a pragmatic problem solver whose impulse upon assuming a new office was to devise and advance new policies. He was less concerned with personal recognition for an action than with getting results. David Potter concludes that Fillmore gets less credit than he deserves for defusing the Texas–New Mexico border dispute he inherited upon taking office. Potter says that Fillmore settled the situation "with such adroitness and seeming ease that history has scarcely recognized the magnitude of his achievement."[14]

Policy Vision

Fillmore held the orthodox Whig commitment to the construction of roads and canals, protective tariffs, and a financial system that fostered economic development. He was unable to win passage of these measures from a Democratic Congress, however. Nevertheless, his highest priority was preserving the Union, which he thought was best served by promoting a compromise that would appeal to both North and South.

Cognitive Style

Fillmore was notable for his cerebral qualities. Webster praised Fillmore as "very diligent, and what he does not know he quickly learns."[15] He was an avid reader who as a young man joined a circulating library to gain access to books and bought a dictionary to look up unfamiliar words. His interest in learning extended to promoting education for others. In the mid-1840s, he helped found the University of Buffalo; as vice president, he took great interest in his role as a member of the board of regents of the Smithsonian Institution; and, as president, he installed the first White House library.

Emotional Intelligence

Fillmore appears to have had a mind-set historian Daniel Walker Howe called the Whig personality, which is marked by a commitment to moderation, self-improvement, and upward social mobility.[16] Biographer Robert J. Rayback remarks that at first he thought of Fillmore as "weak and pompous," but then he concluded that Fillmore "possessed extraordinary strength of character."[17] He is typically described as stolid, bland, and conventional, but such terms underestimate the forcefulness evinced by his handling of the Texas–New Mexico border crisis, his decision to replace Taylor's entire cabinet, and his effectiveness in advancing the Compromise of 1850.

Figure 5.1. Franklin Pierce's charm and good looks helped him win friends from an early age, and he knew how to take a magisterial pose. But these traits did not prepare him for the burdens of the presidency in a time of crisis. Source: Library of Congress, LC-USZ62-13014.

CHAPTER 5

Franklin Pierce and
the Kansas-Nebraska Act

An intriguing paradox characterizes Franklin
Pierce's administration: on the one hand few
administrations exerted such a powerful impact
on the social and political life of the American
nation, but on the other hand few presidents
exercised such little influence on their administration's policies. Pierce was an inconsequential
charmer who staked his claim for presidential
greatness on other people's not very charming
initiatives.

> —William W. Freehling, "Franklin
> Pierce," in Henry F. Graff, ed.,
> *The Presidents: A Reference History*[1]

I believe that the constituted authorities of this
Republic are bound to regard the rights of the
South in this respect as they would view any other
legal and constitutional right, and that the laws to
enforce them should be respected and obeyed, not

with a reluctance encouraged by abstract opinions
as to their propriety in a different state of society,
but cheerfully and according to the decisions of the
tribunal to which their exposition belongs.... I
fervently hope that the question is at rest, and that
no sectional or ambitious or fanatical excitement
may again threaten the durability of our institu-
tions or obscure the light of our prosperity.
—Franklin Pierce, Inaugural Address,
March 4, 1853[2]

The policy of my Administration will not be
controlled by any timid forebodings of evil from
expansion. Indeed, it is not to be disguised that
our attitude as a nation and our position on the
globe render the acquisition of certain possessions
not within our jurisdiction eminently important
for our protection.
—Franklin Pierce, Inaugural Address,
March 4, 1853[3]

FRANKLIN PIERCE WAS THE DARKEST of dark horses.
He won the Democratic Party's 1852 presidential
nomination after a forty-eight ballot impasse in which
none of the party's top three leaders was able to mus-
ter the two-thirds vote needed to become the Democratic flag bearer. A gregarious nonentity, he took
office amid growing anger over the Fugitive Slave Act
and passed on to his successor an acutely polarized

nation. Pierce's historical reputation is captured in a survey of sixty-four historians conducted by C-SPAN in which he ranked fortieth in a field of forty-two.[4]

FORMATIVE YEARS AND POLITICAL ASCENT

Franklin Pierce was born on November 23, 1804, in Hillsborough, New Hampshire. He was the son of Benjamin Pierce and Anna Kendrick Pierce. Benjamin Pierce had been a decorated officer in the Revolution who had fought in the battles of Bunker Hill and Ticonderoga and endured the winter Washington's army spent at Valley Forge. He went on to become a general in the New Hampshire militia, a member of the state legislature, and a two-term governor.

Young Franklin Pierce began school in Hillsborough, went on to attend two local academies, and then transferred to Phillips Exeter Academy. After that, he entered Bowdoin College in Brunswick, Maine, from which he graduated in 1824. During his time at Bowdoin, Pierce and his friends often exchanged rounds of drinks in a local tavern, which appears to have been the beginning of a lifelong addiction to alcohol. Most of Pierce's biographers hold that his alcohol addiction had no bearing on how he conducted his presidency, but the susceptibility to other people's initiatives referred to in the first epigraph of this chapter is consistent with a syndrome known as the alcoholic personality, a personality type marked by the need to please others.[5]

After graduating from Bowdoin, Pierce attended law school in Massachusetts, was admitted to the bar, and then embarked on his political career. In 1828 he was elected to the lower house of the New Hampshire legislature, serving until 1833, including one term as Speaker. He was elected in 1832 to the House of Representatives and went to Washington the next year.

In 1834, while he was in the House, Pierce married the former Jane Means Appleton. They were to have three children, none of whom lived to see their father in the White House. The Pierce marriage was a union of opposites. He not only was a heavy drinker but also was highly gregarious and reveled in politics. She was a temperance advocate, tended to be a social isolate, and abhorred politics. Not surprisingly, she played no part in her husband's administration, depriving him of the independent point of view provided by some presidential wives.[6]

In 1836, after Pierce served two terms in the House, the New Hampshire legislature elected him to the U.S. Senate. Historian William F. Freehling says of Pierce's congressional service that "he made not one noteworthy speech, sponsored not one important bill, emerged not once from the shadows of the congressional hanger-on. He was known chiefly for being the congressman least able to hold his liquor."[7] Most of the friends he made in Congress were Southerners. Chief among them was Mississippi's Jefferson Davis, who later served in Pierce's cabinet and still later was president of the Confederacy.

Pierce's lackluster congressional career came to a close in 1842, when he resigned from the Senate, evidently out of the desire to extricate himself from the alcohol-laced Washington subculture. He returned to New Hampshire to practice law, but he remained active in Democratic politics and was the party leader in his state. He also served briefly as a militia general in the Mexican-American War, though two untimely injuries and an illness prevented him from leading his troops into battle and left him with an undeserved reputation for cowardice.

In June 1852 the Democrats convened in Baltimore to select their presidential candidate. After multiple roll calls, it became evident that none of the major contenders would be able to command support from two-thirds of the delegates because of deep sectional differences. On the forty-ninth ballot, the convention resolved the deadlock by choosing the affable Pierce, who had no enemies and no record on the question of the extension of slavery into territories, the issue that

Figure 5.2. Even in a hard-drinking age, Franklin Pierce was dogged by stories of excessive drinking. In this cartoon, Pierce, holding a bottle, needs the support of a tree to remain upright. In the speech bubble, he curses the state of Maine, which the year before the cartoon's appearance had passed the country's first temperance law. Source: Library of Congress, LC-USZ61-99.

divided party factions. He and his wife were vacationing in Massachusetts at the time of the convention. When informed of the nomination, historian Michael Holt writes, "Pierce seemed stunned. Jane fainted dead away."[8]

Pierce's Whig opponent was General Winfield Scott, the standard-bearer of an even more fragmented party. Whigs mocked Pierce's service in the Mexican-American War and lampooned him as "the hero of many a well-fought bottle."[9] Despite these attacks,

Pierce won an electoral landslide (254 electoral votes to Scott's 42) though he received only 51 percent of the popular vote. Horace Greeley's *New York Tribune* greeted his election with a scathing appraisal: "We have fallen on great times for little men."[10] Pierce took office with his Democratic Party holding a two-thirds majority in the House and more than 60 percent of the Senate. He became the youngest president to date, and he would prove himself not up to the job.

During the interval between Election Day and Inauguration Day, the Pierces experienced a grievous loss. The train car they were riding in was derailed, and their eleven-year-old son Benny's skull was crushed before their eyes. Devastated by the death of their third and last child, Jane Pierce sank into a deep depression, went into isolation, and wore mourning during her husband's presidency. After a visit to Washington, Nathaniel Hawthorne—a Bowdoin classmate and close friend of Pierce—referred to Jane Pierce as "that death's head."[11]

A Pliable Chief Executive

Pierce's inaugural address foreshadowed many of his presidential policies. With American acquisition of Cuba—a step favored by Southerners—in mind, he signaled his support for national expansion by declaring that "timid forebodings of evil" would not deter his administration from acquiring new territory. Pierce may, as some suggest, have taken this stance in the hopes that expansion would unite the country, but such a view was shortsighted: acquisition of Cuba was chiefly a Southern goal.

The new president stated the principle underlying his eventual vetoes of nine welfare and public works bills when he declared that he opposed federal activities not explicitly provided for in the Constitution. He also proclaimed his devotion to the Union, which he called a "radiant constellation," and denounced the "spirit of sectionalism and uncharitableness." Pierce then made plain his view that, in protesting enforcement of the Fugitive Slave Act, the North was chiefly responsible for the present national tension, that slavery was guaranteed under the Constitution, and that laws to support Southern rights "should be respected and obeyed … cheerfully."

One of the few successes of the Pierce presidency related to foreign affairs. Reflecting his expansionist aims, he completed the Gadsden Purchase—obtaining from Mexico land in what is now southern Arizona and New Mexico. Even that success was incomplete, however. Pierce had hoped to purchase much more Mexican territory, but James Gadsden, his minister to Mexico, had to accept the smaller area. Nor did the agreement win immediate approval in Congress. The Senate failed to ratify in its first vote and approved the treaty only after reducing the amount of land acquired still further.

One of Pierce's two great failures was also in the realm of foreign policy. In 1854 Secretary of State William L. Marcy instructed the American ministers to France, Great Britain, and Spain to formulate a policy toward the Spanish colony of Cuba. It was of particular interest to the South to add Cuba to the Union because doing so would extend the domain of slavery. Convening in Ostend, Belgium, the ministers drafted a confidential memorandum that called for the purchase of Cuba by the United States. Under some conditions, they added, the United States would be justified in "wresting" Cuba from Spain. When the so-called Ostend Manifesto became public, there was an outburst of indignation in the North. Labeled a "manifesto of brigands" by critics, the document had to be repudiated by the damaged Pierce administration. The president, who had appointed the diplomats and allowed a rabid Southern expansionist to take part in the meeting, bears some responsibility for the fiasco.[12]

Pierce's second great failure resulted from his endorsement of the Kansas-Nebraska Act, a measure sponsored by Senator Stephen A. Douglas of Illinois.[13] The purpose of the act was to organize territorial government in the northern part of the Louisiana Purchase. Passing such a bill, Douglas knew, required Southern support. That support, in turn, would not be forthcoming unless slavery was permitted in the territory. But the area was north of the upper limit permitted for slavery under the Missouri Compromise of 1820. The only way to allow slavery there was to repeal the Missouri Compromise—on which point Southern lawmakers insisted. Douglas reluctantly agreed, remarking that he expected "a hell of a storm" to break out.* He correctly feared—as did Pierce—that many in the North would see repudiation of the Missouri Compromise as an outrage.

To keep Northern Democrats in line, Douglas concluded, he needed the president's support. He turned to one of the Southern members of the cabinet, Secretary of War Jefferson Davis, to arrange a meeting between Pierce and the advocates of the Kansas-Nebraska bill. The day before that meeting, Pierce discussed repealing the Missouri Compromise with his cabinet. Only Davis and the other cabinet secretary from the South favored doing so. The remainder of the group advised against it, arguing that it would be

---

* Douglas's original bill adopted the popular sovereignty language of the acts organizing New Mexico and Utah with no direct position on the Missouri Compromise. Southerners pushed him to revise the bill several times until he had to repeal explicitly the Missouri Compromise line.

more prudent to seek a court ruling on the matter, pointing out that the Southern-dominated Supreme Court would be likely to declare the compromise of 1820 unconstitutional. The effect, they reasoned, would be the same, but the administration could avoid being damaged as it would by becoming directly involved in the repeal.

Pierce seemed to have been persuaded by this reasoning—until the following day, when the meeting with the advocates of repeal took place. Of its nine participants, only Douglas and Pierce were Northerners. While the precise content of their discussion is not known, this much is certain. By its end, Pierce had reversed course. Despite his cabinet's warnings, he would throw his support behind abandonment of the Missouri Compromise. He apparently asked the Southerners and Douglas to meet with a cabinet member highly skeptical of the move. They made an attempt that failed, and Pierce did not press the matter further.

Douglas's bill put the issue of slavery in the territories in the hands of the majority of territorial residents, following the principle of popular sovereignty. Congress wrangled bitterly over the bill for nearly four months, but it finally passed. Roll-call votes showed how divisive the measure was for Northern Democrats in the House, who split nearly evenly on it.

The Whigs, on the other hand, divided along sectional lines. Nine of the eleven Southern Whigs in the Senate and thirteen of twenty-four Southern Whigs in the House voted in favor of the bill, which passed the House by precisely thirteen votes.

Once the Kansas-Nebraska Act was on the books, armed pro- and antislavery settlers raced to occupy Kansas. Rival constitutions were framed, and Kansas exploded in violence. Not only had sectional tension triumphed over compromise, but bitter feelings had led to bloodshed.

Why was Pierce so unwise? Various reasons have been given, none of them mutually exclusive. Some historians hold that he was too weak to resist the phalanx of repeal advocates. Others take the view that, dedicated to party unity, he went along with Douglas and powerful Southern congressional leaders. Still others say that he accepted Douglas's argument that the bill would cause Democrats to close the ranks by clearly distinguishing their support for popular sovereignty as opposed to Whig intransigence against it. While he undoubtedly had political goals in mind, Pierce's shift may well have been related to his apparent alcoholic personality. All of the explanations point to the lack of wisdom in his action.

Pierce hoped to win his party's nomination a second time, but word of the fighting in Kansas began to appear as the Democrats met in their national nominating convention in 1856. Four years of poor leadership combined with news of blood on the Plains convinced the Democrats that selecting the incumbent as their standard-bearer would be unwise. Pierce thus became the first incumbent president rejected by his own party. He retired, spending two years in Europe and then settling again in New Hampshire, where he opposed Lincoln's emancipation policy and treatment of Copperheads, mourned the death of his wife, supported Andrew Johnson's Reconstruction policies, and continued to drink heavily.

LEADERSHIP QUALITIES

Public Communication

Franklin Pierce gets poor grades as a public communicator. His official messages were verbose, as exemplified by his wordy inaugural address, but also unpersuasive because they lacked depth and penetration. Pierce was also doubly hurt by the rise of independent newspapers and his own ineffectual control of the *Washington Union*, the Democratic Party organ. In contrast to Polk's effective management of his newspaper, Pierce was confronted by editorials in the so-called administration paper that countered his positions and reflected the agendas of other party leaders.[14]

Organizational Capacity

Pierce's affability enabled him to preside over the longest-lasting cabinet to date in American history, and William Freehling gives him good marks for making cabinet selections aimed at healing party differences. Nevertheless, he did not use his associates to good effect. The circumstances around his endorsement of the Kansas-Nebraska bill continue to be instructive. After seeming to accept his cabinet's advice not to advance it, Pierce reversed course the next morning. He compounded the problem by not ensuring that those in favor of the bill meet with cabinet members and bring them into line. In short, he was able to maintain harmony in his cabinet, but he failed to use the group effectively.

Political Skill

As discussed in chapter 1, political skill may be tactical or strategic. Franklin Pierce clearly lacked either skill, as is evident from the political fiascos that punctuated his presidency. Pierce was ill served by a prepresidential career during which he had been an undistinguished member of Congress and a party operative rather than an elected official. If Pierce had spent more time running for office and less in the backrooms of his party, he might have had a better understanding of political feeling across the nation and thus spared himself the anger that resulted from repealing the Missouri Compromise. The times required an adept politician and strong leader. Pierce—a "soothing mediocrity"[15]—was neither. As with Polk, Pierce's effectiveness can be judged in part in election results. The Kansas-Nebraska Act he supported seriously damaged the Democratic Party in the North. Northern Democrats lost sixty-six of ninety-one seats in the House in the elections that followed passage of that act. This act also played a significant role in the creation and rapid rise of the Republican Party.

Policy Vision

Pierce's policy vision was grounded in Jacksonian democracy. Indeed, his commitment to the views of "Old Hickory" led him to be dubbed the "Young Hickory of the Granite Hills of New Hampshire." Thus, his interpretation of the Constitution was narrow and rigid, a view that led him to veto more bills than all but two of his predecessors. Pierce's first veto illustrates his inflexibility. He negated a bill designed by an early champion of the rights of the disabled that would have authorized the funding of asylums for the indigent insane. The measure was backed by a wide spectrum of the political community, including Pierce himself. Nevertheless, he vetoed it on the grounds that the bill's purpose was not explicitly provided for in the Constitution.

Cognitive Style

By one criterion, Pierce can be said to have had a powerful mind, as is evinced by his ability to deliver his inaugural address from memory. But by a far more important yardstick, his mind was flawed. Like Polk, he was not far seeing enough to anticipate the fallout from a particular action, in his case repealing the Missouri Compromise. In sum, his mind performed well on details but was deficient in understanding the big picture.

Emotional Intelligence

Franklin Pierce may not have been the least emotionally intelligent president in American history. He was less troubled than Richard Nixon, whose emotional flaws destroyed his presidency, or Bill Clinton, whose sexual adventures nearly ruined his. Still, he appears to have been an alcoholic, he exceeded others in the rigidity of his interpretation of the Constitution, and he lacked the fortitude to resist face-to-face political pressure. None of this behavior speaks well for his emotional intelligence, and much of it is consistent with the medical literature on alcoholism.[16]

Figure 6.1. James Buchanan's characteristic head tilt, visible here, resulted from having a disorder in one eye. To some, the attitude gave him an air of courtesy. To others, it was another sign of a somewhat fussy personality. "Old Buck's" inability to see clearly with both eyes was reflected in his one-sided view of the sectional crisis. Source: Library of Congress, LC-BH82101-6628.

~ CHAPTER 6 ~

The Disastrous Presidency of James Buchanan

Few Presidents have assumed public office with a more distinguished record of public service than James Buchanan [and] few have experienced such devastating political defeats or adopted policies that were so self-defeating. Buchanan left office abandoned by his friends and scorned by his enemies and with the nation on the brink of civil war.

> —William E. Gienapp,
> "James Buchanan: 1857–1861," in
> Alan Brinkley and Davis Dyer, eds.,
> *The Reader's Companion to the American Presidency*[1]

All agree that under the Constitution slavery in the States is beyond the reach of any human power except that of the respective States themselves wherein it exists.

> —James Buchanan, Inaugural
> Address, March 4, 1857[2]

The immediate peril arises ... from the fact that the incessant and violent agitation of the slavery question throughout the North for the last quarter of a century has at length produced its malign influence on the slaves and inspired them with vague notions of freedom. Hence a sense of security no longer exists around the family altar. This feeling of peace at home has given place to apprehensions of servile insurrections. Many a matron throughout the South retires at night in dread of what may befall herself and children before the morning. Should this apprehension of domestic danger ... extend and intensify itself until it shall pervade the masses of the Southern people, then disunion will become inevitable.

—James Buchanan, Fourth Annual Message to Congress, December 3, 1860[3]

LIKE FRANKLIN PIERCE, James Buchanan was a Northern politician with Southern principles—a common phenomenon of the Civil War era. He had been a presence in American politics for more than four decades when he assumed the presidency. It was widely expected that his extensive political experience would enable him to reverse the spiral of conflict between the free and slave states, but when he stepped down, several Southern states had left the Union and war was imminent, in no small part because of his pro-Southern policies.

FORMATIVE YEARS
AND POLITICAL RISE

Buchanan was born on April 23, 1791, in the vicinity of Harrisburg, Pennsylvania, to James Buchanan Sr., and Elizabeth Speer Buchanan. After studying at a school near his home, Buchanan attended Pennsylvania's Dickinson College, from which he graduated with honors. He went on to study law and in 1812 was admitted to the bar. Buchanan is the only American president who never married. Early in his legislative career, he was engaged, but his fiancée broke off the engagement and then died, and he remained a bachelor. As will be seen, the lack of a true life partner might have had an effect on Buchanan's ability to handle the pressures of office.[4]

From his election to the Pennsylvania state legislature in 1815 until the end of his presidency in 1861, James Buchanan was almost continuously in public office. Between those two points, he also served in both houses of Congress, as minister to Russia during the Jackson presidency, as secretary of state in the Polk administration, and as minister to Great Britain during the four years that preceded his own presidency.*

Buchanan's experience in the last of these positions helps explain his selection at the 1856 Democratic nominating convention. In a party split by sectional divisions, he became the compromise candidate because, since he had been out of the country, he had not taken a position on the explosive issue of the extension of slavery into Kansas and Nebraska.

Buchanan won the presidency in a three-way contest in which he was opposed by the growing Republican Party's John C. Frémont and the anti-immigrant Know-Nothing party's Millard Fillmore. Buchanan received 174 electoral college votes with 45 percent of the popular vote, Frémont won 114 electoral votes and 33 percent of the popular vote, and Fillmore managed 8 electoral votes on 22 percent of the popular vote. Buchanan's victory was closer than it seemed. He won only five Northern states, including his home state of Pennsylvania, where he barely managed a majority.

Buchanan spent much of the period between his election and his inauguration selecting what may well be the most ideologically one-sided cabinet in the nation's history. Four of its seven members were

---

* Not surprisingly, he was known as "Old Public Functionary."

Southern slaveholders; two were Northerners who, like Buchanan, were sympathetic to the South; and the final one was too aged to play an effective role. He hurt his own chances for political success by refusing to include anyone from the Northern wing of the Democratic Party led by Illinois senator Stephen A. Douglas, whom Buchanan disliked, both personally and politically.

Buchanan in the White House

In his inaugural address, Buchanan described the debate over the extension of slavery to the territories as "a matter of but little practical importance" because the Supreme Court was about to settle the issue once and for all. Two days later, Chief Justice Roger B. Taney handed down the sweeping *Dred Scott* decision, which declared that Congress had no constitutional power to exclude slavery from anywhere in the nation and that blacks "had no rights which the white man was bound to respect."

Buchanan had reason to know what the Court's ruling would be when he delivered his inaugural. Informed in advance of the decision, he had secretly (and illegitimately) persuaded Justice Robert Grier, a fellow Pennsylvanian, to concur, adding a Northern

OUR NATIONAL BIRD AS IT APPEARED WHEN HANDED TO JAMES BUCHANAN.MARCH.4.1857.

THE IDENTICAL BIRD AS IT APPEARED A.D. 1861.

Figure 6.2. A Republican cartoon from 1861 ridicules the administration of James Buchanan, who became president of a strong nation in 1857, represented by the eagle on the left, but bequeathed to his successor a weakened, downcast nation, damaged by "anarchy" and "secession." Source: Michael Angelo Woolf, *Our National Bird as It Appeared When Handed to James Buchanan, March 4, 1857. The Identical Bird as It Appeared, A.D. 1861.* New York: Thomas W. Strong. 1861. Courtesy of Archives and Special Collections, Dickinson College, Carlisle, PA.

voice to the Southern majority. Buchanan's inaugural wishful thinking notwithstanding, slavery remained a burning issue. Northerners were incensed at the Court's ruling. Poet and editor William Cullen Bryant pointedly asked, "Are we to accept … that hereafter it shall be a slaveholders' instead of the freemen's Constitution?" Bryant's answer was an emphatic "Never! Never!"[5]

The lack of any entanglement in the furor over the Kansas-Nebraska Act had been one of Buchanan's principal attractions to the Democrats, but his absence from the country during the bitter debate over that law and the aftermath may have crippled him politically. As William E. Gienapp observes, Buchanan "had not witnessed firsthand the angry sectional passions aroused by the Kansas-Nebraska Bill, did not comprehend the situation in Kansas, and failed to grasp the reasons for the Republican party's success."[6] That unfamiliarity may have led to his first major decision, a blunder. Buchanan supported the proslavery state constitution promulgated in the town of Lecompton, Kansas, even after it became evident that an overwhelming majority of Kansans opposed permitting slavery in the territory—and over the objections of the man he himself had appointed as territorial governor.

Buchanan's decision proved politically disastrous. Despite his offers of patronage and other inducements to win votes in Congress to approve the Lecompton constitution, the House refused to comply and asked Kansans to vote on the constitution again.* Meanwhile, the Kansas fiasco had been costly to the Demo-

---

*In August of 1858, Kansans voted overwhelmingly against the Lecompton constitution. Soon after, they approved an antislavery constitution, though Southern Democrats blocked admission of Kansas as a state. Statehood finally occurred in 1861, when, after secession of the South, Republicans controlled both houses of Congress.

cratic Party. In the 1858 elections, half the Northern Democrats lost their seats, costing the party its House majority. Significantly, anti-Lecompton Democrats, backed by Douglas, did better than Democrats who had voted with the administration.[7]

At this point, Buchanan might have patched up his differences with Douglas in an effort to restore party unity. Instead, he punished the senator and his supporters further. The administration systematically replaced any holder of a patronage job who was connected to the anti-Lecompton Democrats. For good measure, Buchanan backed a move by Southern Democratic senators to replace Douglas as chairman of the committee on territories, a position he had held for a decade.

The conflict over slavery effectively blocked action on anything else in the second half of Buchanan's term. The president, at any rate, did not advance any significant domestic legislative proposals, though he did attempt some foreign policy initiatives. He responded to political turmoil in Mexico by asking Congress for troops and funds in effect to create an American-controlled zone in northern Mexico and requested $30 million to try to buy Cuba from Spain. Both these initiatives were principally backed by Southerners in Congress, further distancing Buchanan from the Northern wing of his party.

By 1860, any attempt to pass legislation was over-whelmed by attention to the coming presidential campaign. The Democratic Party fractured along sectional fault lines. Southern delegates unwilling to accept Douglas as the nominee walked out of the national convention and chose their own candidate, while the remaining Democrats chose the Illinois senator. Republican Abraham Lincoln won a four-candidate election.

Late that year, as several Southern states threatened to act on the oft-spoken threat to secede, Buchanan delivered his final message to Congress. In it, he blamed disunion entirely on the North: the cause of secession, he said, is "the long-continued and intemperate interference of the Northern people with the question of slavery in the Southern States."[8] He then met the crisis imperiling the nation by speaking out of both sides of his mouth. First, at great length, he advanced the strict constitutionalist view that secession was illegal. Then, he argued that neither president nor Congress had any constitutional power to stop it. Finally, he concluded that it would be folly to resist secession:

> The fact is that our Union rests upon public opinion, and can never be cemented by the blood of its citizens shed in civil war. If it can not live in the affec-

tions of the people, it must one day perish. Congress possesses many means of preserving it by conciliation, but the sword was not placed in their hand to preserve it by force.[9]

Faced with the dissolution of the Union, Buchanan rejected the strong stands taken by Andrew Jackson in the nullification crisis and by Zachary Taylor in 1850 and did nothing.

Buchanan was devastated by secession, suffering an emotional collapse that forced him to preside over some of his cabinet meetings from his bed. By the time he stepped down, the North had lost all the federal forts in the seceding states except Fort Sumter in South Carolina and three in Florida. After endorsing an abortive effort to reinforce the garrison at Sumter, Buchanan made no further moves to resist secession.

During the 1856 presidential campaign, Buchanan had told an associate, "No competent and patriotic man to whom [the presidency] may be offered should shrink from the responsibility, yet he may well accept it as the greatest trial of his life."[10] Relieved that his trial had finally ended, on the day of Abraham Lincoln's inauguration in 1861, a weary Buchanan told the incoming president, "If you are as happy in entering the White House as I shall feel on returning [home] to Wheatland, you are a happy man indeed."[11]

Buchanan undeniably was dealt a difficult hand. Nevertheless, he played it poorly. Historian Jean Harvey Baker delivers a plausible judgment on Buchanan's four years as president:

> Granting that he faced many challenges brought on by intensifying division between the North and South, reasonable Americans of all parties still had cause to expect that if anyone could quiet the passions of sectionalism, it would be the Sage of Wheatland. Instead, Buchanan's presidency demonstrated the harm that can result when great talent and experience are shackled to a personality ill suited to the pressures of the office.[12]

As soon as he left office, Buchanan yearned to publish a history of his administration that would justify his decisions. Advised not to do so until the Civil War was over, Buchanan labored long on his book and chafed at the delay in its publication until 1866. Sadly for the former president, the memoir did not provide the hoped-for vindication. Beginning with a *New York Times* review that dismissed Buchanan as "self-apologist for his own imbecile and disastrous administration," critics scorned the work and its author.[13] Buchanan died two years later.

Leadership Qualities

Public Communication

In his official messages, Buchanan's style was verbose and pedantic. In addition, while he tried to promote national unity, his message was unremittingly pro-Southern and marred by unsupported claims and fuzzy thinking.

As a veteran politician, Buchanan was familiar with the nineteenth-century presidential practice of communicating with the public by means of a subsidized newspaper. However, he occupied the White House during a period in which it had become difficult for a president to communicate in this manner. Congress had begun to control printing contracts, and presidents could no longer be sure of having an official mouthpiece. The rise of a more independent mass-circulation press and professional journalists was a further impediment.

Had he been a more effective communicator, Buchanan might have been able to persuade the journalists of the day of the merits of his policies. Try as he might, though, Buchanan was unable to persuade them that such policies as supporting the blatantly biased Lecompton constitution had merit.[14]

Organizational Capacity

Buchanan chose an egregiously pro-Southern cabinet. For much of his presidency, he met daily with his this group, oblivious to the perils of receiving one-sided advice that conformed to his own way of thinking. As a lonely bachelor, he made the cabinet his principal source of social support as well, dining with its members and their wives. Buchanan even urged cabinet members to spend the night at the White House when their wives were out of town. The result was that he was ensconced in what now would be referred to as a "bubble," cut off from any independent sources of advice.

While Buchanan has been accused of being dominated by his cabinet, that characterization misses the mark. He had strongly held views; it just happens that they were the same as those of most of his cabinet. Indeed, rather than manipulating him, his cabinet was somewhat deferential to him. That deference exacerbated the problem of living in the bubble.

Political Skill

No one with as extensive a political career as Buchanan could have been devoid of political skill. He was not the weak president he is often portrayed to be. He had his goals, and he tried to achieve them. For example, Buchanan tried to use every means possible—including, some reports said, providing female companions to wavering legislators—to win congressional approval of the Lecompton constitution. He was also highly resourceful in his feud with Stephen Douglas by using the patronage weapon and helping strip the senator of his committee chairmanship. But in a larger sense, it was not an act of skill for Buchanan to embark on a vendetta against the most prominent leader of one wing of his party. Indeed, that feud hurt both his presidency and his party. In short, he was tactically skilled but strategically lacking in skill.

More significantly, Buchanan had little feel for the political pulse of the nation during his presidency. Michael Birkner suggests that one reason for Buchanan's failure is that he came to the office too late in his career and thought in terms of the older Jacksonian-Whig conflict rather than in terms of the newer conflict between free and slave states:

> Probably under different circumstances—for example, during the mid-1840s—Buchanan could have been a successful president. He had the skills, if not the vision, to be a very good president. But he was too old, too ill, too poorly leveraged in the late 1850s to serve effectively. He was representative of an increasingly

unstable and unpopular Jacksonian political order, working with tools unequal to the task he faced.[15]

Policy Vision

Buchanan was most notable for his lack of policy vision. Indeed, he often took both sides of issues, as he did on the legality of secession. His political flexibility first became evident in the 1820s, when this one-time Federalist became a Jacksonian Democrat. Polk noted the same quality when Buchanan served as his secretary of state, recording in his diary that his adviser had at one point adopted a more aggressive position on the Oregon issue in order to enhance his chances to gain the White House.

Buchanan presented himself as a statesman but was never strongly identified with any cause or issue. As Allan Nevins puts it in describing his prepresidential career, "No great law, dramatic event, no revealing speech, was associated with his name."[16] That was not the case when he left office; his presidency will be forever linked to the secession winter and his failure to do anything about it. As with Polk and Pierce, Buchanan's lack of policy vision rendered him unable to see clearly that his actions—in his case, his support for the Lecompton constitution—would further inflame sectional conflict.

Cognitive Style

Buchanan's intellectual qualities are well illustrated in his writings. Consider, for example, his four annual messages to Congress. They were prolix, legalistic, and laden with unsupported assertions, such as the outlandish claim in his third annual message that slaves in the American South were "well fed, well clothed, and not over worked" and lived in good conditions due to the "philanthropy and the self-interest" of their owners. That passage also reveals how thoroughly he sympathized with Southern ideas. So, too, did his tendency to lump anyone with the slightest reservation on the issue of the expansion of slavery with the most extreme abolitionists and his denunciation of all abolitionists as troublemakers.

Emotional Intelligence

In her biography of Buchanan, Jean Baker asserts that Buchanan's more problematic actions—including his support of the proslavery Lecompton constitution despite its overwhelming unpopularity with the people of Kansas, his failure to act when South Carolina initiated secession, and his failure to defend Fort Sumter early—resulted from his lack of emotional intelligence, which she says manifested itself in his "arrogant wrongheaded, uncompromising use of power."[17] To what extent Buchanan's inability to control his emotions resulted from his lack of the emotional support of a spouse remains an open question. What is clear is that, at a fundamental level, Buchanan lacked the emotional fortitude to stand up to the pressures of being a chief executive. When strong national leadership was needed, he lacked the fiber to confront the situation, taking to his bed.

Figure 7.1. Abraham Lincoln, in this famous last photograph taken in February 1865, shows the cares of nearly four years of war etched on his nearly fifty-six-year-old face. The man whom many reviled as a gorilla early in his presidency had proven himself a resolute, skillful, remarkably humble leader. Photo by Alexander Gardner. Source: Library of Congress, LC-USZ62-8812.

CHAPTER 7

Abraham Lincoln: Consummate Leader

The ant [that] has toiled and dragged a crumb to his nest will furiously defend the fruit of his labor against whatever robber assails him.... The most dumb and stupid slave who has ever toiled for a master does constantly *know* that he is wronged.... Although volume upon volume is written to prove slavery a very good thing, we never hear of the man who wants to take the good of it *by being a slave himself*.

> —Abraham Lincoln, Fragment on Slavery, circa July 1, 1854[1]

I state my general idea of this war to be that we have the greater numbers, and the enemy has the greater facility of concentrating forces upon points of collision.... We must fail unless we can find some way of making our advantage an over-match for his; and this only can be done by menacing him with superior forces at different points at the same time.

> —Abraham Lincoln, Letter to
> Brigadier General Don Carlos Buell,
> January 13, 1862[2]

With malice toward none; with charity for all, with firmness in the right, as God gives us to see the right, let us strive on to finish the work we are in, to bind up the nation's wounds, to care for him who shall have borne the battle and for his widow and his orphan, to do all which may achieve and cherish a just and lasting peace among ourselves and with all nations.

> —Abraham Lincoln, Second
> Inaugural Address, March 4, 1865[3]

ABRAHAM LINCOLN AND JAMES BUCHANAN were light years apart in their political credentials. Lincoln entered the White House following a mere eight years as a state legislator and two years in the House of Representatives. Buchanan took the presidential oath after more than four decades in public office, during which he served as a state legislator, member of both houses of Congress, secretary of state, and minister to both Russia and Great Britain. Yet Lincoln ranked first in a poll of historians on presidential performance conducted in 2009, and Buchanan ranked last.[4]

Formative Years and Political Rise

Abraham Lincoln was born on February 12, 1809, in a log cabin in the Kentucky wilderness. Although his parents, Thomas Lincoln and the former Nancy Hanks, were semiliterate, he educated himself, borrowing books from his neighbors. He also read the King James Bible and drew on its imagery and cadences in many of his speeches. Lincoln's mother died when he was nine. His stepmother, the former Sarah Bush Johnston, encouraged him greatly in his studies.

During Lincoln's childhood, his family moved first to Indiana and then to Illinois. In 1831 he struck out on his own, settling in the hamlet of New Salem, where he worked as a store clerk, postmaster, and surveyor. Lincoln was much admired by his neighbors for his honesty, amiability, and willingness to help others. He also stood out for his exceptional height and strength, qualities much valued on the frontier.

Not long after arriving in New Salem, Lincoln announced his candidacy for the state legislature.[5] Unfortunately for him, he was soon called to serve three months in the Illinois militia, leaving him little time to campaign. He ran eighth in the only election in which he lost the popular vote, though he received 277 of the 300 votes cast in New Salem. Two years later, when he was better known throughout the entire legislative district, Lincoln was elected to the first of four terms. As being a legislator was then a part-time occupation, Lincoln turned to the law as a source of income. He read law on his own and passed the bar in 1836.

In 1842 Lincoln married Mary Todd. Todd, from a prosperous and well-connected family, was a good catch for the up-and-coming lawyer. The differences between the two were striking. Abraham was "disorganized, careless in dress, and indifferent to social niceties," while Mary "dressed expensively and lived by the strict decorum of Victorian conventions." Abraham "got along with almost everybody," but Mary "quarreled with servants, workmen, merchants, and some of Lincoln's friends."[6] It has been argued that Lincoln's difficult marriage affected his leadership by increasing his forbearance.

Lincoln had a complex and elusive personality. He periodically sank into deep depressions that were relieved by telling anecdotes and jokes, which he described as the "vents" of his "moods and gloom."[7]

With the Whigs in the minority in Illinois, Lincoln stood no chance of winning higher state office. He therefore set his sights on the congressional seat in his district. He helped broker an agreement in which the district's Whigs would rotate service in Washington. In 1846 it was Lincoln's turn. His congressional service coincided with the Mexican-American War. Like other Whigs, he opposed the war, holding that President Polk had embarked on it under false pretenses in order to seize territory from a weaker nation, a point he made clear in a January 1848 speech dissecting and dismissing Polk's territorial claims. Lincoln returned home at the end of his term and began to practice law with renewed energy.

Path to the Presidency

In the spring of 1854, Lincoln was drawn back into politics by the passage of the Kansas-Nebraska Act. That fall, as Senator Stephen A. Douglas traversed Illinois defending the law, Lincoln dogged his footsteps, countering the Democrat's arguments and honing his own message against the expansion of slavery.

In an October 1854 speech in Peoria, Lincoln gave the first of a series of addresses on the morality of slavery that were to catapult him to the presidency. Declaring that he hated the Kansas-Nebraska Act because it left open the possibility that a state might opt for slavery, Lincoln made the following assertion:

> I hate it because it deprives our republican example of its just influence in the world—enables the enemies of free institutions ... to taunt us as hypocrites

..., causes the real friends of freedom to doubt our sincerity and especially because it forces so many really good men amongst ourselves into an open war with the ... principles of the Declaration of Independence.[8]

Thinking that a majority of the new Illinois state legislature would support an anti-Kansas-Nebraska Act candidate, Lincoln entered the running for a U.S. Senate seat in 1856. Unable to win the votes he needed from anti-Kansas-Nebraska Democrats, Lincoln withdrew in favor of one of those Democrats. After that election, Lincoln left the Whig Party and joined the newly formed antislavery Republican Party.

In 1858 Lincoln again ran for the Senate. This time his opponent was Douglas, seeking a third term. The two candidates staged a series of debates across the state in which they wrestled over many issues, primarily the extension of slavery. While voters sent a Democratic majority to the state house that returned Douglas to the Senate, the debates won Lincoln newfound prominence, which bore fruit in 1859. He was invited to give a speech in New York. Addressing an audience of influential easterners, Lincoln focused his remarks on the immorality of slavery. The address was received with such acclaim that he set his sights on the presidency.[9]

Figure 7.2. Cartoonist Frank Bellew of *Harper's Weekly* drew the implications of Lincoln's 1864 reelection and the Republican gains in Congress: the tall president grew taller with voters' endorsement of his war and emancipation policies. Source: *Harper's Weekly*, "Long Abraham Lincoln a Little Longer," Nov. 26, 1864, p. 768. Reproduced courtesy of HarpWeek, LLC.

Lincoln's managers devised a strategy for winning the Republican nomination, aided by the fact that the party convention would, conveniently, take place in Chicago. It worked as planned. After the four leading candidates canceled one another out on the first two ballots, Lincoln won the nomination on the third. In a similar dynamic, Lincoln won the presidency in a four-candidate race by winning an overwhelming majority of the electoral college despite having only 40 percent of the popular vote—a tiny minority of which came from slave states. In the months following his election, seven Southern states seceded from the Union and formed the Confederate States of America. Lincoln would preside over a divided nation.

White House Years

By the time of his inauguration, Lincoln had made his cabinet selections, choosing (and, in effect, neutralizing) his rivals for the nomination. Much of Lincoln's inaugural address was devoted to reassuring the South that he had no intention of interfering with slavery where it already existed. While describing secession as "the very essence of anarchy," he concluded with a plea to the South:

> I am loath to close. We are not enemies, but friends. We must not be enemies. Though passion may have

strained, it must not break our bonds of affection. The mystic chords of memory, stretching from every battlefield and patriot grave to every living heart and hearthstone all over this broad land will yet swell the chorus of the Union, when again touched, as surely they will be, by the better angels of our nature.

The next day, Lincoln was informed that the besieged garrison of Fort Sumter, in the harbor of Charleston, South Carolina, was running out of supplies. After much reflection, he decided to resupply it but without using force. The onus would thus be on the South to initiate any violence. On April 12, before the supplies arrived, the Confederates opened fire on the fort, and the Civil War had begun.

Lincoln quickly called seventy-five thousand state militiamen into federal service, instituted a naval blockade of the South, and suspended the right of habeas corpus in the corridor between Philadelphia and Washington. He also called a special session of Congress for July 4, which gave him almost three months during which he could use his power as commander in chief to conduct the war.

Lincoln's call for troops sent four more states into the Confederacy. One of his pressing concerns, then, was retaining Delaware, Kentucky, Maryland, and Missouri, where slavery was also legal. Lincoln therefore took such actions as revoking a military order that would have freed the slaves in Missouri to avoid alienating its slaveholders.[10]

Lincoln was also preoccupied with finding a general in chief who would prosecute the war with sufficient vigor. The need for such a commander was made urgent by a steady string of Confederate victories in the eastern theater of the war well into 1863. Lincoln tried and then relieved several generals before giving overall command of the army to Ulysses S. Grant, who had enjoyed success in the western theater.

Lincoln was the model of a hands-on commander in chief. He immersed himself in books on military strategy and, as shown by the second epigraph to this chapter, enunciated the strategy that led to victory, insisting that the Union use its superior resources to press the Confederate forces on a wide front until it found a weak spot where it could break through.

In July 1862 Lincoln decided it would be necessary to free the slaves in the rebel states to deprive the Confederacy of an important asset. Soon after, he convened his cabinet and read a draft emancipation proclamation to it. Explaining that he had made up his mind on the substance of the matter, Lincoln requested advice on how best to carry it out. He accepted the recommendation of Secretary of State William Seward that he wait for a Union victory before announcing the policy to avoid giving the impression of acting out of desperation.

Turn of the Tide

In September 1862 Union forces halted a Confederate invasion of the North in the Battle of Antietam. A few days later, Lincoln issued a preliminary statement declaring that by the end of the year the slaves would be freed in any rebel states that did not rejoin the Union. As none of the Southern states complied, on January 1, 1863, he signed the Emancipation Proclamation. Freeing the slaves helped prevent the South from gaining the recognition and assistance it sought from European powers.

The Battle of Antietam was a harbinger of future Union victories. In July 1863 another Southern invasion of the North was blocked in the Battle of Gettysburg. The next day, the surrender of Vicksburg gave the Union effective control of the Mississippi River. In the course of 1864, Grant's forces fought relentlessly in the east against those of Confederate general Robert E. Lee. Meanwhile, another army under William Tecumseh Sherman captured Atlanta and went on to march through Georgia to the coast.

Lincoln was renominated early in June of that year. The Democratic candidate was General George B. McClellan, who had at one point commanded all the Union armies. Lincoln's running mate was Andrew Johnson of Tennessee, a leading pro-Union Southern Democrat. Lincoln was reelected with a margin of some 400,000 popular votes and 212 of the 233 electoral college votes.

Lincoln's second inaugural address was steeped in religious imagery. "Fondly do we hope, fervently do we pray," he declared, "that this scourge of war may speedily pass away." Yet it might be God's will, he continued, that the conflict would not end "until all the wealth piled by the bondsman's two hundred and fifty years of unrequited toil shall be sunk, and until every drop of blood drawn with the lash shall be paid by another drawn with the sword."[11]

Lincoln had only six more weeks to live. On April 9, the war effectively came to a close with Lee's surrender in Virginia. On April 14, the Lincolns attended a play at Washington's Ford's Theater. Actor John Wilkes Booth, a Confederate sympathizer, entered their box and shot Lincoln in the head at close range. He died the following morning without regaining consciousness.

There is no way of knowing what would have occurred had Lincoln not been killed, but there can be no doubt that his death had profound consequences. Had he lived, the nation might have been spared the traumatic course of the Reconstruction that followed the war.[12] As it was, Lincoln's successor, Andrew Johnson, reversed Lincoln's policy toward the South by failing to stand up for the rights of African Americans and allowing all but a few former Confederates to immediately reenter public life. Republican radicals in Congress responded by enacting punitive Reconstruction policies that included military occupation of the South. Eventually, though, Northern interest in Reconstruction waned, and the former slave owners regained power and enacted laws depriving African Americans of their rights, a state of affairs that continued until the civil rights movement of the 1950s.

LEADERSHIP QUALITIES

Public Communication

Abraham Lincoln excelled in all of the qualities used here to assess leadership. In the realm of communication, he showed acumen in the way he managed his message, the vision conveyed in his statements, and the clarity of his rhetoric.

Lincoln effectively managed communications. His telling impromptu speeches to soldiers during visits to army encampments might have contributed to building the bond that led the majority of the troops to vote for his reelection in 1864. He also skillfully revealed or concealed his policies as occasion demanded, as evidenced by the cagey way he handled questions during the interregnum between his election and inauguration and by his handling of Horace Greeley's August

1862 open letter urging him to adopt an emancipation policy. Lincoln responded to Greeley with an open letter of his own stating his personal abhorrence of slavery and explaining that he would free none, some, or all the slaves depending on which action contributed most to the overarching goal of restoring the Union. Adroitly, though, he did not let on that he had already decided to adopt the policy because he was not ready to say so.

Lincoln's national vision is best revealed by his two inaugural addresses and the Gettysburg Address, three models of oratory. The first inaugural, quoted earlier, reveals Lincoln's devotion to the principles of the Declaration of Independence and vision of a shared American identity. The second, part of which serves as the third epigraph to this chapter, offers a vision of reconciliation that might have been possible to achieve only under the leadership of such a president as he.

As for Lincoln's rhetorical skill, honed by years of effort, it is instructive to compare Seward's draft of Lincoln's first inaugural address with Lincoln's markup of it:

> SEWARD: We are not, we must not be, aliens or enemies, but fellow-countrymen and brethren.

> LINCOLN: We are not enemies, but friends. We must not be enemies.

SEWARD: Although passion has strained our bonds of affection too hardly, they must not, I am sure they will not, be broken.

LINCOLN: Though passion may have strained, it must not break our bonds of affection.[13]

Organizational Capacity

Lincoln's organizational methods were unsystematic but effective. They were driven by his political acumen. The best example is his decision to include his four rivals for the 1860 Republican nomination in his cabinet, which discouraged them from criticizing his policies. More importantly, it afforded him the advice of able political leaders and—because of their diversity of views—ensured that cabinet debates would be spirited and instructive. He could be something of a micromanager, though he was willing to delegate authority when he found aides in whom he could place his trust. Salmon P. Chase, his secretary of treasury, effectively financed the war with little interference from Lincoln. Once he found Grant, he had a general in whom he had complete confidence.

Political Skill

Lincoln was a master politician who could cooperate with others regardless of their viewpoints. He also excelled at gauging and shaping public opinion, plumbing the character of others, and weighing policy alternatives and anticipating their consequences. Lincoln was effective, too, in outmaneuvering others without alienating them. He adeptly moved his first secretary of war, Simon Cameron, out of the cabinet when Cameron's corruption became problematical by naming Cameron as minister to Russia. Similarly, he defused a potential cabinet crisis caused by Chase and later packed the treasury secretary off to the Supreme Court. Modern presidents would do well to take him as a role model.[14]

Policy Vision

Lincoln once declared that he was controlled by events and had no underlying political agenda. However, he was a dedicated Whig for most of his career and then became an equally dedicated Republican. As such, he favored a wide range of policies designed to advance economic development.* Though Lincoln suspended habeas corpus, he also embraced the Constitution, insisting on allowing the 1864 election to be held de-

---

* Major domestic achievements on Lincoln's watch included the Homestead Act, which made extensive western land available for settlement; the Land-Grant College Act, which provided land grants to states that created agricultural colleges; and the Pacific Railroad Acts, which provided for the nation's first transcontinental railroad, not to speak of the sheer accomplishment of conducting a free and fair election in wartime.

spite the ongoing war. As a Republican, he was committed to the halting slavery's expansion; when he determined that emancipation would promote restoration of the Union, he embraced that policy. While he detested slavery and showed no signs of racial prejudice in his interactions with African Americans, he did believe that the best solution for emancipated slaves was for them to colonize another country. In this, his otherwise clear vision was clouded by the thinking of his times.

Cognitive Style

Lincoln was noteworthy for his clarity of mind. He made every effort to sharpen his legal reasoning, including teaching himself Euclidean geometry. His mastery of the law demonstrates the depth of his mind; his ability to grasp the principles of military strategy and shows its breadth. As the insight implied in the first epigraph to this chapter reveals, he had a knack for stripping away false arguments or confusing details and discovering the heart of an issue. He often expressed those insights in the form of a joke, a practice that excited much disapproval from politicians or generals who had narrow points of view; were afflicted by self-importance; or were, quite simply, humorless. The clarity with which he saw issues is also revealed in such masterpieces of concision as the Gettysburg Address and his first and second inaugurals.

Emotional Intelligence

Lincoln's political style was grounded in an emotional intelligence that he forged in his battle against what was then called melancholia. Historian Michael Burlingame effectively brings out many of Lincoln's psychological complexities in a volume that reviews such seeming pathology as his recurrent depressions but concludes in the final paragraph of his book that Lincoln was a "model of psychological maturity."[15]

CHAPTER 8

What Difference Did the President Make?

Had the United States possessed three farseeing,
imaginative, and resolute presidents instead of
Fillmore, Pierce, and Buchanan, the [Civil] War
might have been postponed until time and
economic forces killed its roots.

—Allan Nevins, *The Statesmanship of
the Civil War*[1]

BY WAY OF CONCLUSION, I return to the issues addressed in this book's introductory chapter. As we have
seen, the Civil War era posed profound challenges to
these six presidents. There is widespread agreement
that Abraham Lincoln met that test in a superlative
manner and that Franklin Pierce and James Buchanan
responded to it abysmally. It is also widely held that
Millard Fillmore's performance was pedestrian and
James K. Polk's was unusually effective. (Taylor served
too briefly to be assessed.) The Civil War era is an

instructive period in which to study presidential effectiveness both because these presidents faced such profound challenges and because they ranged so widely in ability that they can be productively compared.

In what follows, I review the way each of these protagonists rose, or failed to rise, to the challenges of his times. I then explore the ways in which the leadership criteria employed in this book figured in the period under consideration. I conclude by discussing a pair of theoretical issues implicit in Allan Nevins's assertion in the epigraph to this chapter that if the nation had "possessed three farseeing, imaginative, and resolute" chief executives "instead of Fillmore, Pierce, and Buchanan, the [Civil] War might have been postponed."

Summing Up the Presidents

James K. Polk (1845–49) was a staunch Jacksonian Democrat who set four major goals for his administration and achieved each one. Polk managed the Mexican-American War effectively, but he failed to anticipate that bitter contention would arise between the North and the South over the status of slavery in the Mexican Cession. Nevertheless, Polk had more accomplishments in a single term than most chief executives have in two.

Zachary Taylor (1849–50) was a rough-hewn professional soldier who made it a matter of principle during his military service to neither vote nor take a public stand on public issues. Though a slave owner, "Old Rough and Ready" angered the South first by advancing a plan for the Mexican Cession that was against its interests and later by threatening to use military force to prevent the South from seceding. Of course, Taylor's plan became moot when he died in the summer of 1850.

Millard Fillmore (1850–53), a moderate Whig, was selected as Taylor's running mate to balance the ticket with a Northerner. He deserves credit for accepting the need for a more evenhanded compromise and energetically working to achieve it. His subsequent actions angered both sections and led his party to deny him a chance for his own race for president.

Franklin Pierce (1853–57) was a Northern politician who supported Southern policies. Such leaders were the adhesive that joined the Northern and Southern wings of the Democratic and Whig parties in the nineteenth century. Despite contrary advice from his cabinet, Pierce succumbed to pressure and used his presidential resources to advance a measure that legalized slavery in areas where it had previously been illegal. In doing so, he helped stoke sectional conflict. His failure is evident in the fact that his party, rather than nominating him for a second term, looked elsewhere.

James Buchanan (1857–61) was another "dough-face," or Northerner with Southern leanings. As one of the nation's most experienced public figures, Buchanan was widely expected to unite the rival forces in the nation. But his decisions were so one-sidedly pro-Southern that he deepened sectional divisions, helping to fracture his own party and promote the rise of an antislavery rival. By the time his term had ended, the seven states of the Deep South had seceded, and the nation was on the brink of war.

Abraham Lincoln (1861–65) is widely acknowledged to be the nation's greatest president. He had the self-confidence to appoint his competitors for the Republican nomination to his cabinet, and he was noteworthy (along with much else) for his sense of timing, persistence in advancing his purposes, and ability to promote them lucidly and with unequaled eloquence. His assassination had far-reaching effects on the course of American history.

Summing Up the Political Qualities

Public Communication

The norm during the Civil War era was for presidents to communicate with the public mainly by issuing official documents and planting stories and editorials in newspapers, rather than by making formal speeches. That norm changed slightly toward the end of the period, with the rise of an independent press and the decline of party newspapers. Polk was most effective in using newspapers as a tool of presidential communication, working closely with his handpicked editor and sometimes placing his, or his cabinet officer's, words in his chosen newspaper. Lincoln had no administration paper but masterfully used interviews with journalists and open letters to convey his message.

Of these six presidents, Lincoln was by far the most effective public communicator. In his long career as a lawyer and in public life, he perfected his prose to become a model of eloquence and conciseness. It is instructive to note that the average length of Lincoln's annual messages to Congress on the state of union—just over 6,800 words—is far less than that of the other five presidents considered here.* He also effectively managed his message, ensuring that he did not reveal too much of his thinking until he judged the time ripe for it.

* Polk tops the list with an average length of 18,014 in his four annual messages to Congress. The verbose Buchanan comes next at 14,097, followed by Fillmore and Pierce at the nearly identical 10,498 and 10,457, respectively. Only Taylor, whose sole annual message was only 7,617 words, comes close to Lincoln, but his brevity results more from his limited view of the president's scope than the desire to keep his cards close to his vest. (These average lengths are taken from the American Presidency Project, http://www.presidency.ucsb.edu/sou_words.php#axzz1mwScpkhm.)

Franklin Pierce and Millard Fillmore anchor the opposite end of the spectrum. Because they had largely been party operatives, Pierce and Fillmore had little sense of how to appeal to the public, and their public addresses were windy, turgid affairs.[2] Buchanan's public communications were wordy and shot through with flawed reasoning that reflected his narrow point of view. Taylor's messages reflected his lack of formal education and singleness of purpose. Polk's formal addresses were long and detailed but often clear and forceful in their expression of his goals and rationale.

Organizational Capacity

The back-to-back presidencies of Lincoln and Buchanan mark the extremes in a number of political qualities, including organizational capacity. Lincoln appointed a cabinet that consisted of his four opponents for the 1860 presidential nomination and included every faction in his party. Buchanan's cabinet was populated by friends and skewed toward the South until the secession crisis. As a consequence, Lincoln was exposed to a rich fare of advice and information, and Buchanan was isolated from the Northern Democrats.

Polk ranks behind Lincoln in effective use of his cabinet. Like Lincoln, he was a strong president who listened to his cabinet's advice but made up his own mind. Fillmore was probably next most effective in using his cabinet, which he chose rather than relying on officials inherited from Taylor. Taylor delegated patronage awards and department responsibilities to his cabinet, reflecting his experience in the army. He leaned on them little for political advice, relying more heavily on the influential Senator William Seward. In his most significant presidential decision, Pierce seemed to accept his cabinet's advice and then abandoned it. The group remained intact throughout his term, but these advisers were an ineffectively used tool in an ineffective presidency.

Political Skill

The least skilled of the Civil War era presidents—Zachary Taylor—had the apt nickname "Old Rough and Ready." Taylor was unbending in his support of his own politically unrealistic plan for addressing an issue that contributed to the growing fissure between the sections. Franklin Pierce also showed little political skill, more influenced by others than being an active puller of political strings. Buchanan was more forceful a president than Pierce, but his attempts to coax Congress to adopt his goals failed miserably and damaged the northern wing of his party.

Fillmore effectively used patronage and party loyalty to help ensure passage of the five bills that made
up the Compromise of 1850. Abraham Lincoln and
James K. Polk were the most skilled presidents of this
period. Polk set a handful of specific goals for his
presidency and bent every effort to bring them into
being, but his skill was merely tactical. He lacked the
strategic vision that would have led him to anticipate
the conflict that arose over the extension of slavery
into the Mexican Cession. Lincoln's vision, on the other
hand, was strategic as well as tactical. He was a master
of the art of the possible but was also able to anticipate
the long-run effects of his policies.

Policy Vision

Skill is not enough for presidential success. That skill
must also be harnessed to a policy vision. There is
nothing more counterproductive than a vision that
has unintended and undesired consequences. Polk's
policy vision was clearly flawed. Contention between
the North and the South over the status of slavery
in the Mexican Cession had the effect of setting the
nation on the path to the Civil War. Taylor, Pierce, and
Buchanan all showed circumscribed vision. Each was
dedicated to preserving the Union but could not craft
policies that would ensure that outcome by satisfying

both North and South—granted that to do so would be a formidable task.

The political agenda of Fillmore, the accidental president, is represented by his leadership in bringing about the Compromise of 1850 and the evenhandedness of his other actions. That his enforcement of both the Fugitive Slave Law and the principle of neutrality alienated both sections highlights the difficult position faced by the chief executives of the 1850s. Lincoln excelled in vision as in the other categories. He articulated a clear goal—to restore the Union—and chose policies depending on how they contributed to that end.

Cognitive Style

The presidencies of Lincoln and Buchanan provide object lessons in cognitive clarity. Buchanan's goals were muddled and self-contradictory—he could not both preserve the Union and support only the Southern view of issues. Lincoln's were crystal clear, as can be seen from the lucidity with which he spelled out an overall war strategy, exceeding most of his generals in the astuteness of his vision. Polk was an incisive thinker whose interest began and ended in politics. Taylor showed some shrewdness in his analysis of the issue of slavery in California and New Mexico but also evinced an inability to recognize the political realities he faced. Fillmore had a sound mind that was, like Lincoln's, largely the result of self-education. Pierce, a good lawyer, could command a multitude of details but was unable to combine them into a larger picture.

Emotional Intelligence

Franklin Pierce provides insight into flawed emotional intelligence. His principal shortcoming was vulnerability to group pressure. Characteristically, Pierce appeared to have accepted his cabinet's advice against backing the divisive Kansas-Nebraska Act only to change course and yield to a largely Southern group that pressured him to back it. Dramatically different was Lincoln, who was susceptible to bouts of melancholy but forged a robust emotional intelligence by coming to terms with this condition.

Polk was seemingly unaware of the debilitating effects of his dedication to work and barely survived his presidency. Taylor could not always control his temper and could be influenced by his tendency to harbor resentment over perceived slights against him. Fillmore expressed his anger at his treatment by Taylor's cabinet by replacing it, but the action was not merely spiteful—he also sought advisers who favored the compromise policy that he supported. Buchanan proved himself as lacking in emotional intelligence as in other leadership qualities. The state of the Union was poor when, in the midst of the secession crisis, the chief executive was so overwhelmed that he took to his bed.

Two Theoretical Issues

As the title of the journal *History and Theory* makes evident, many issues dealt with by historians are theoretical rather than factual. I conclude with observations on two such matters—the utility of counterfactuals and the construct known as the funnel of causality.

Counterfactuals are assertions contrary to fact, such as the statement by Allen Nevins quoted as the chapter's epigraph. As Tim De Mey and Eric Weber put it, counterfactuals "are at once *fictional*, since they invariably start from states of affairs that didn't really happen, and *useful* (perhaps sometimes even indispensable)" in historical analysis.[3]

The Civil War era was punctuated with episodes in which the question of who occupied what position lends itself to counterfactual reasoning. Consider the election of 1844. If James K. Polk had not narrowly defeated Henry Clay that year, it is unlikely that the Mexican-American War would have occurred. In that case, the United States probably would not have acquired the Mexican Cession, and the conflict between the North and the South over the status of slavery within those lands would not have occurred.*

By the same logic, if Zachary Taylor had not died in the summer of 1850, the grand compromise of that year probably would not have been made. In that event, several historians have argued, Taylor's emphatic rejection of Southern threats to secede would have prevented the nation's breakup or—in Holman Hamilton's words—"would have defeated secession, rebellion, civil war, or challenges to federal authority under any other name."[4] Similarly, if the weak, Southern-leaning Franklin Pierce had not been Fillmore's successor, it is unlikely that the Kansas-Nebraska Act would have been passed.

Had James Buchanan not won the 1856 election and pursued the Lecompton constitution, the Union may well not have been dissolved. Buchanan's extreme pro-Southern tilt helped promote the growth of the Republican Party while also severely weakening the Democratic Party in the North. That weakness contributed to the Republican victory in 1860. Another counterfactual redounds more in Buchanan's favor.

---

* The Mexican Cession would probably have remained Mexican for two reasons. First, Clay had no interest in going to war for that land. Second, had there been no Mexican-American War, gold would have been discovered in 1848 in Mexican California. The government of Mexico would hardly have been willing to let go of the area in that case.

Had Buchanan not been pushed by new, antisecession cabinet members, he might have yielded Fort Sumter and other federal forts to the Confederacy. While such an action would not have made the outbreak of war any less likely, it might have forced Abraham Lincoln to make a more aggressive move that would have put an entirely different stamp on the opening of hostilities and thus on the way the war effort was perceived in the North, in the border states, and around the world.

Finally, if Abraham Lincoln had not been assassinated, the nation might have been spared the trauma of Reconstruction. Lincoln had shown himself during the war to be masterful at managing the more fervid congressional Republicans and at setting the agenda for the war. While Reconstruction would draw less upon his powers as commander in chief—and thus was open to more congressional influence in policy making—Lincoln would undoubtedly have done a better job than Andrew Johnson in shaping that policy.

These counterfactuals establish that the men who occupied the White House in the Civil War era and what they did while there made a difference. What Alan Brinkley and Davis Dyer say more generally of the nation's chief executives is clearly true of this sextet: "Understanding the presidency requires, of course, taking seriously the role that individuals play in history; and there are many occasions in which one could imagine a very different history if a different leader had been in place."[5]

The *terms levels of analysis* and *funnel of causality* have been used to account for the seeming contradiction that both particular sociopolitical conditions *and* presidents and other historical actors can correctly be said to have caused the Civil War.[6] As Michael Lewis-Beck and his associates put it, the funnel of causality is a metaphor "that provides a useful way to think about the causal process."[7] The large mouth of the funnel represents such background factors as the different interests of the slave and free states and their disagreement over such issues as the extension of slavery into the Mexican Cession. Its narrow stem represents the much more constricted decision environment faced by later individuals, most notably Abraham Lincoln and Jefferson Davis, who became president of the Confederacy.

There have been endless claims and counterclaims over the years about the causes of the Civil War. By and large, they boil down to two assertions: One, the war was the result of such background conditions as slavery and the divergent economic systems of the North and the South; the other, the war resulted from the actions taken by Northern and Southern political leaders up to and including Lincoln and Davis.[8]

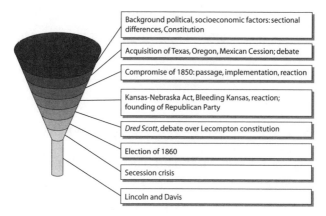

Figure 8.1. The Funnel of Causality.

While such assertions cannot be *re*solved by historical inquiry, the construct in Figure 8.1 suggests that they can be *dis*solved by analytical clarification. The first assertion refers to determinants found at the top of the metaphorical funnel. The second refers to those at its stem. What appears to be an argument over matters of fact proves to be a debate over two categories of determinants—background events or conditions that create the environment in which people, including public officials, act and those immediate causes that appear at its outlet. Both sets of determinants were factors in the eventual outcome, but those at the top are far enough away from the funnel's spout that they permitted a variety of outcomes. As events piled on events, however, choices became more narrow until, at the bottom of the funnel, actors had fewer options. Lincoln no longer could choose compromise as earlier presidents had done. He had to accept the fact of secession or oppose it.

A Coda on the Presidential Difference

It is a near truism that political (and other) behavior is a function of individual actors and the environments in which they act.[9] It is also well known that there are particular conditions under which individuals are likely to have a major impact on events, including situations that are ambiguous, that are new or volatile, and that can be considered tipping points.[10] Moreover, some people are more likely than others to make a difference, including those who are well placed in decision-making processes, who are highly motivated, and who have distinctive strengths or crippling weaknesses.[11]

From these contingences, it is not surprising to find that the presidents of the Civil War era—in the midst of a volatile political environment, at the pinnacle of executive power, in some cases driven by ambitious goals, and both deeply gifted and seriously flawed—played a crucial part in the history of the nation. To paraphrase the old spiritual, they had the whole wide nation in their hands.

Background on the Civil War Era Presidents

JAMES K. POLK, 11TH PRESIDENT (1845–1849)

Life

Birth Date: November 2, 1795
Birthplace: Mecklenburg County, N.C.
Parents: Samuel Polk, Jane Knox
Religion: Presbyterian
College Education: University of North Carolina
Wife: Sarah Childress
Date of Marriage: January 1, 1824
Children: None

Political Party: Democratic

Other Positions Held:
> Member, Tennessee House of Representatives (1822–1825)
> Member, U.S. House of Representatives (1825–1839)
> Speaker, U.S. House of Representatives (1835–1839)
> Governor, Tennessee (1839–1841)

Date of Inauguration: March 4, 1845
End of Term: March 5, 1849

Date of Death: June 15, 1849
Place of Death: Nashville, Tenn.
Place of Burial: Nashville, Tenn.

Elections: Candidates, Party, Electoral Vote, and Percentage of Popular Vote

ELECTION OF 1844

James K. Polk, Democratic, 170, 50%
Henry Clay, Whig, 105, 48%
James G. Birney, Liberty, 0, 2%

DID NOT RUN IN ELECTION OF 1848

VICE PRESIDENT

George M. Dallas (1845–1849)

Political Composition of Congress

29TH CONGRESS (1845–1847)

Senate: Democrat 34; Whig 22; vacant 2
House: Democrat 142; Whig 79; American (Know-Nothing) 6

30TH CONGRESS (1847–1849)

Senate: Democrat 38; Whig 21; Independent Democrat 1
House: Whig 116; Democrat 110; Independent Democrat 2; American (Know-Nothing); Independent 1

Appointments

CABINET

James Buchanan, secretary of state (1845–1849)
William L. Marcy, secretary of war (1845–1849)

Cave Johnson, postmaster general (1845–1849)
Robert J. Walker, secretary of the treasury (1845–1849)
John Y. Mason, attorney general (1845–1846)
Nathan Clifford, attorney general (1846–1848)
Isaac Toucey, attorney general (1848–1849)
George Bancroft, secretary of the navy (1845–1846)
John Y. Mason, secretary of the navy (1846–1849)

SUPREME COURT

Levi Woodbury (1845–1851)
Robert C. Grier (1846–1870)

Key Events

1845   U.S. Naval Academy opens (October 10); Texas admitted to Union (December 29).

1846   Congress declares war on Mexico (May 13); Senate ratifies treaty with Great Britain over Oregon question (June 18); Congress passes Polk's tariff bill (July 29); Polk vetoes internal improvements bill, angering Northern Democrats (August 3); Polk signs into law the independent ("constitutional") treasury system, an alternative to having a central bank (August 6); Pennsylvania Representative David Wilmot introduces his "proviso" banning slavery from any territory acquired as a result of the Mexican-American War (August 8); Smithsonian Institution established (August 10); Iowa admitted as state (December 28).

1847   General Zachary Taylor defeats superior Mexican force at Battle of Buena Vista (February 22–23); first Mormons reach Great Salt Lake area in Mormon migration to Utah (July 22); General Winfield Scott captures Mexico City (September 14).

1848   Gold discovered in California (January 24); gold rush begins as word of the discovery spreads; Treaty of Guadalupe Hidalgo ends Mexican War (February 2); Wisconsin admitted as state (May 29); Seneca Falls Convention for women's rights (July 19–20); in annual message to Congress, Polk confirms the discovery of gold in California (December 5); first gas lamps and improved central heating system installed in White House.

1849   Department of Interior established (March 3).

ZACHARY TAYLOR, 12TH PRESIDENT (1849–1850)

Life

Birth Date: November 24, 1784
Birthplace: Near Barboursville, Va.
Parents: Richard Taylor, Sarah Dabney Strother
Religion: Episcopalian
College Education: None
Wife: Margaret Mackall Smith
Date of Marriage: June 21, 1810
Children: Ann Mackall, Sarah Knox, Octavia Pannill, Margaret Smith, Mary Elizabeth, Richard

Political Party: Whig

Other Positions Held:
>   First Lieutenant, U.S. Army (1809–1810)
>   Captain, U.S. Army (1810–1812, 1815)
>   Major (Brevet), U.S. Army (1812–1815)
>   Major, U.S. Army (1816–1819)
>   Lieutenant Colonel, U.S. Army (1819–1832)
>   Colonel, U.S. Army (1832–1838)
>   Brigadier General, U.S. Army (1838–1846)
>   Major General, U.S. Army (1846–1849)

Date of Inauguration: March 5, 1849
End of Term: July 9, 1850 (died in office)

Date of Death: July 9, 1850
Place of Death: Washington, D.C.
Place of Burial: Near Louisville, Ky.

Elections: Candidates, Party, Electoral Vote, and Percentage of Popular Vote

ELECTION OF 1848

Zachary Taylor, Whig, 163, 47.5%
Lewis Cass, Democratic, 127, 42.5%
Martin Van Buren, Free-Soil, 0, 10%

VICE PRESIDENT

Millard Fillmore (1849–1850)

Political Composition of Congress

31ST CONGRESS (1849–1851)

Senate: Democrat 35; Whig 25; Free-Soil 2
House: Democrat 113; Whig 108; Free-Soil 9; American (Know-Nothing) 1; Independent 1

Appointments

CABINET MEMBERS

John M. Clayton, secretary of state (1849–1850)
George W. Crawford, secretary of war (1849–1850)
Jacob Collamer, postmaster general (1849–1850)
Thomas Ewing, secretary of the interior (1849–1850)
William M. Meredith, secretary of the treasury (1849–1850)
Reverdy Johnson, attorney general (1849–1850)
William B. Preston, secretary of the navy (1849–1850)

None

Key Events

1849   California adopts free state constitution (October 13) and soon after applies for statehood.

1850   U.S. population: 23,191,876; Henry Clay argues in Senate for his compromise proposal (February 5–6); Virginia senator James Mason delivers John C. Calhoun's speech denouncing Clay's compromise plan, as Calhoun is too ill to speak for himself (March 4); Calhoun dies (March 31); Clay introduces compromise measures as a single "Omnibus" bill (May 8); Nashville Convention meets, rejects Clay's compromise calls for extension of Missouri Compromise line to the Pacific Ocean (June 3–12); New Mexico voters approve a free-state constitution (June 20); Taylor signs Clayton-Bulwer Treaty, calling for joint U.S.-British control of a canal across Central American isthmus (July 5); Taylor becomes second president to die in office (July 9).

MILLARD FILLMORE, 13TH PRESIDENT
(1850–1853)

Life

Birth Date: January 7, 1800
Birthplace: Summerhill, N.Y.
Parents: Nathaniel Fillmore, Phoebe Millard
Religion: Unitarian
College Education: None
First Wife: Abigail Powers (died 1853)

Date of First Marriage: February 5, 1826
Children from First Marriage: Millard Powers, Mary
    Abigail
Second Wife: Caroline Carmichael McIntosh
Date of Second Marriage: February 10, 1858
Children from Second Marriage: None

Political Party: Whig

Other Positions Held:
    Member, New York State Assembly (1828–1831)
    Member, U.S. House of Representatives (1833–
    1835, 1837–1845)
    Comptroller, New York State (1847)
    Vice President (1849–1850)

Date of Inauguration: July 10, 1850 (succeeded to presi-
    dency on death of Zachary Taylor)
End of Term: March 4, 1853
Date of Death: March 8, 1874
Place of Death: Buffalo, N.Y.
Place of Burial: Buffalo, N.Y.

Elections

RAN AS VICE PRESIDENT IN 1852
(SEE TAYLOR FOR RESULTS)

DID NOT RUN IN ELECTION OF 1852

VICE PRESIDENT

None

Political Composition of Congress

31ST CONGRESS (1849–1851)

Senate: Democrat 35; Whig 25; Free-Soil 2

House: Democrat 113; Whig 108; Free-Soil 9; American (Know-Nothing) 1; Independent 1

32ND CONGRESS (1851–1853)

Senate: Democrat 36; Whig 23; Free-Soil 3
House: Democrat 127; Whig 85; Unionist 10; Free-Soil 4; Independent Democrat 3; States Rights 3; Independent Whig 1

Appointments

CABINET MEMBERS

John M. Clayton, secretary of state (1850)
Daniel Webster, secretary of state (1850–1852)
Edward Everett, secretary of state (1852–1853)
George W. Crawford, secretary of war (1850)
Charles M. Conrad, secretary of war (1850–1853)
Jacob Collamer, postmaster general (1850)
Nathan K. Hall, postmaster general (1850–1852)
Samuel D. Hubbard, postmaster general (1852–1853)
Thomas Ewing, secretary of the interior (1850)
Thomas M. T. McKennan, secretary of the interior (1850)
Alexander H. H. Stuart, secretary of the interior (1850–1853)
William M. Meredith, secretary of the treasury (1850)
Thomas Corwin, secretary of the treasury (1850–1853)
Reverdy Johnson, attorney general (1850)
John J. Crittenden, attorney general (1850–1853)
William B. Preston, secretary of the navy (1850)
William A. Graham, secretary of the navy (1850–1852)
John P. Kennedy, secretary of the navy (1852–1853)

SUPREME COURT

Benjamin Robbins Curtis (1851–1857)

Key Events

1850   "Omnibus" version of Compromise of 1850 collapses in Senate in a flurry of votes over conflicting amendments (July 31); Fillmore signs into law five statutes admitting California as a free state, organizing New Mexico and Utah territories with no restrictions as to slavery, toughening treatment of fugitive slave cases, and ending the slave trade in the District of Columbia (September 9–20); second women's rights convention held, in Worcester, Massachusetts (October 23–24); White House library established.

1851   *Uncle Tom's Cabin* by Harriet Beecher Stowe begins serialized publication (June 5).

1852   Commodore Matthew C. Perry leaves on expedition to "open" Japan (November).

1853   Washington Territory separated from Oregon Territory (March 3).

FRANKLIN PIERCE, 14TH PRESIDENT
(1853–1857)

Life

Birth Date: November 23, 1804
Birthplace: Hillsborough (now Hillsboro), N.H.
Parents: Benjamin Pierce, Anna Kendrick
Religion: Episcopalian
College Education: Bowdoin College
Wife: Jane Means Appleton
Date of Marriage: November 19, 1834
Children: Franklin, Frank Robert, Benjamin

Political Party: Democratic

Other Positions Held:
> Member, New Hampshire House of Representatives (1829–1833)
>
> Speaker, Hew Hampshire House of Representatives (1831–1832)
>
> Member, U.S. House of Representatives (1833–1837)
>
> Member, U.S. Senate (1837–1842)
>
> Brigadier General, U.S. Army (1847)

Date of Inauguration: March 4, 1853
End of Term: March 4, 1857
Date of Death: October 8, 1869
Place of Death: Concord, N.H.
Place of Burial: Concord, N.H.

Elections: Candidates, Party, Electoral Vote, and Percentage of Popular Vote

ELECTION OF 1852

Franklin Pierce, Democratic, 254, 51%
Winfield Scott, Whig, 42, 44%
John P. Hale, Free-Soil, 0, 5%

DID NOT RUN IN ELECTION OF 1856

VICE PRESIDENT

William Rufus de Vane King (1853) (died in office)

Political Composition of Congress

33RD CONGRESS (1853–1855)

Senate: Democrat 38; Whig 22; Free-Soil 2
House: Democrat 157; Whig 71; Free-Soil 4; Independent Democrat 1; Independent 1

34TH CONGRESS (1855–1857)

Senate: Democrat 39; Opposition 21; American (Know-Nothing) 1; Republican 1

House: Opposition 100; Democrat 83; American (Know-Nothing) 51

Appointments

CABINET MEMBERS

William L. Marcy, secretary of state (1853–1857)
Jefferson Davis, secretary of war (1853–1857)
James Campbell, postmaster general (1853–1857)
Robert McClelland, secretary of the interior (1853–1857)
James Guthrie, secretary of the treasury (1853–1857)
Caleb Cushing, attorney general (1853–1857)
James C. Dobbin, secretary of the navy (1853–1857)

SUPREME COURT

John Archibald Campbell (1853–1861)

Key Events

1853   Gadsden Purchase signed, settling boundary question with Mexico for $10 million (December 30); first hot water piping installed in White House living quarters.

1854   Commodore Perry signs Treaty of Kanagawa with Japanese officials (March 31); Kansas-Nebraska Act signed into law organizing the territories with popular sovereignty and repealing Missouri Compromise (May 30); Ostend Manifesto written (October 18); Democrats suffer heavy losses in congressional elections (November); fighting erupts in Kansas; Republican Party begins to form in re-action to Kansas-Nebraska Act.

1855   Pressure from armed proslavery men in Kansas forces territorial legislature to pass proslavery laws (March); antislavery forces in Kansas adopt To-peka Constitution (August); Native American Party (Know-Nothing Party) takes the name American Party (June 5); fighting in Kansas continues.

1856   Fighting in Kansas continues.

1857   Kansas adopts proslavery Lecompton constitu-tion when antislavery residents abstain from vot-ing (September).

JAMES BUCHANAN, 15TH PRESIDENT
(1857–1861)

Life

Birth Date: April 23, 1791
Birthplace: Cove Gap (near Mercersburg), Pa.
Parents: James Buchanan, Elizabeth Speer
Religion: Presbyterian
College Education: Dickinson College
Wife: Never married

Political Party: Democratic

Other Positions Held:
Member, Pennsylvania House of Representatives (1815–1816)
Member, U.S. House of Representatives (1821–1831)
U.S. Minister to Russia (1832–1834)
Member, U.S. Senate (1834–1845)
Secretary of State (1845–1849)
U.S. Minister to Great Britain (1853–1856)

Date of Inauguration: March 4, 1857
End of Term: March 4, 1861
Date of Death: June 1, 1868
Place of Death: Near Lancaster, Pa.
Place of Burial: Lancaster, Pa.

Elections: Candidates, Party, Electoral Vote, and Percentage of Popular Vote

ELECTION OF 1856

James Buchanan, Democratic, 174, 45%
John C. Frémont, Republican, 114, 33%
Millard Fillmore, American (Know-Nothing), 8, 22%

DID NOT RUN IN ELECTION OF 1860

VICE PRESIDENT

John C. Breckinridge (1857–1861)

Political Composition of Congress

35TH CONGRESS (1857–1859)

Senate: Democrat 41; Republican 20; American (Know-Nothing) 5
House: Democrat 132; Republican 90; American (Know-Nothing) 14; Independent Democrat 1

36TH CONGRESS (1859–1861)

Senate: Democrat 38; Republican 26; American (Know-Nothing) 2
House: Republican 116; Democrat 83; Opposition 19; Anti-Lecompton Democrat 8; Independent Democrat 7; American (Know-Nothing) 5

Appointments

CABINET MEMBERS

Lewis Cass, secretary of state (1857–1860)
Jeremiah S. Black, secretary of state (1860–1861)
John B. Floyd, secretary of war (1857–1860)
Joseph Holt, secretary of war (1861)
Aaron V. Brown, postmaster general (1857–1859)
Joseph Holt, postmaster general (1859–1861)
Horatio King, postmaster general (1861)
Jacob Thompson, secretary of the interior (1857–1861)
Howell Cobb, secretary of the treasury (1857–1860)
Philip F. Thomas, secretary of the treasury (1860–1861)
John A. Dix, secretary of the treasury (1861)
Jeremiah S. Black, attorney general (1857–1860)
Edwin M. Stanton, attorney general (1860–1861)
Isaac Toucey, secretary of the navy (1857–1861)

SUPREME COURT

Nathan Clifford (1858–1881)

Key Events

1857   Supreme Court issues *Dred Scott* decision, ruling
        that African Americans are not U.S. citizens and
        cannot sue in federal courts and that Congress
        cannot ban slavery from territories (March 6);
        Kansans approve Lecompton constitution in fraud-
        ulent election (December 21); Panic of 1857 fol-
        lows boom after Mexican-American War.

1858   Kansans reject Lecompton constitution in a sec-
        ond, fairer vote (January 4); Senate approves Le-
        compton constitution, but House rejects it, send-
        ing the issue back to Kansas (May 4); Minnesota

admitted as state (May 11); Lincoln-Douglas Debates (August 21–October 15).

1859   Oregon admitted as state (February 14); Kansas residents approve new antislavery constitution (October 4); John Brown's Raid: Brown seizes the Harper's Ferry, Virginia, armory and is captured by marine force under Colonel Robert E. Lee (October 16–18); Brown hanged for treason (December 2); Comstock Lode of silver deposits discovered in Virginian City, Nev.

1860   U.S. population: 31,443,321; Davis Resolutions: Jefferson Davis introduces in Senate slavery resolutions banning personal liberty laws and preventing territorial residents from banning slavery (February 2); Lincoln gains recognition for Cooper Union speech on extension of slavery and popular sovereignty (February 27); First Democratic Convention: after days of wrangling in Charleston, party splits over platform, nominee and Southern delegates walk out (May 3); Constitutional Union convention: formers Whigs and American (Know-Nothing) Party members meet in Baltimore and nominate John Bell on moderate, Unionist platform (May 9); Republican Convention: in Chicago, Republicans nominate Lincoln (May 18); Sectional Democratic Conventions: Northern Democrats meet in Baltimore and nominate Stephen A. Douglas while Southern Democrats meet separately and nominate John J. Breckinridge (June 23); Lincoln elected president (November 6); South Carolina secedes from the Union (December 20).

1861   Ship fails to deliver needed supplies to Union garrison at Fort Sumter (January 9); Secession: Mississippi, Florida, Alabama, Georgia, Louisiana, and

Texas leave Union (January 9–February 1); Kansas admitted as a state (January 19); seceded states meet in Montgomery, Alabama, to adopt constitution of Confederate States and name Jefferson Davis president (February 4–9); Davis inaugurated as presidents of Confederacy (February 18).

ABRAHAM LINCOLN, 16TH PRESIDENT
(1861–1865)

Life

Birth Date: February 12, 1809
Birthplace: Hardin (now Larue) County, Ky.
Parents: Thomas Lincoln, Nancy Hanks
Religion: No denomination
College Education: None
Wife: Mary Todd
Date of Marriage: November 4, 1842
Children: Robert Todd, Edward Baker, William Wallace, Thomas ("Tad")

Political Party: Republican

Other Positions Held:
>Member, Illinois General Assembly (1834–1841)
>Member, U.S. House of Representatives (1847–1849)

Date of Inauguration: March 4, 1861
End of Term: April 15, 1865 (assassinated by John Wilkes Booth)
Date of Death: April 15, 1865
Place of Death: Washington, D.C.
Place of Burial: Springfield, Ill.

Elections: Candidates, Party, Electoral Vote, and Percentage of Popular Vote

ELECTION OF 1860

Abraham Lincoln, Republican, 180, 40%
Stephen A. Douglas, Democratic, 12, 29%
John C. Breckinridge, Democratic, 72, 18%
John Bell, Constitutional Union, 39, 13%

ELECTION OF 1864

Abraham Lincoln, Union, 212, 55%
George B. McClellan, Democratic, 21, 45%

VICE PRESIDENTS

Hannibal Hamlin (1861–1865)
Andrew Johnson (1865)

Political Composition of Congress

37TH CONGRESS (1861–1863)

Senate: Republican 31; Democrat 15; Unionist 3
House: Republican 108; Democrat 44; Unionist 26; Constitutional Unionist 2; Union 2; Independent Democrat 1

38TH CONGRESS (1863–1865)

Senate: Republican 33; Democrat 10; Unconditional Unionist 5; Unionist 4
House: Republican 85; Democrat 72; Unconditional Unionist 16; Unionist 9; Independent Republican 2

Appointments

CABINET MEMBERS

William H. Seward, secretary of state (1861–1865)
Simon Cameron, secretary of war (1861–1862)
Edwin M. Stanton, secretary of war (1862–1865)
Montgomery Blair, postmaster general (1861–1864)
William Dennison, postmaster general (1864–1865)
Caleb B. Smith, secretary of the interior (1861–1863)
John P. Usher, secretary of the interior (1863–1865)
James Harlan, secretary of the interior (1865)
Salmon P. Chase, secretary of the treasury (1861–1864)
William P. Fessenden, secretary of the treasury (1864–1865)
Hugh McCullough, secretary of the treasury (1865)
Edward Bates, attorney general (1861–1864)
James Speed, attorney general (1864–1865)
Gideon Welles, secretary of the navy (1861–1865)

SUPREME COURT

Noah Haynes Swayne (1862–1881)
Samuel Freeman Miller (1862–1890)
David Davis (1862–1877)
Stephen Johnson Field (1863–1897)
Salmon Portland Chase, Chief Justice (1864–1873)

Key Events

1861   Lincoln inaugurated (March 4); Civil War begins with Confederate firing on Fort Sumter and surrender of Union garrison (April 12–13); Lincoln declares that a state of insurrection exists and calls for militia (April 15); Secession: Virginia, Arkansas, North Carolina, and Tennessee secede (April 17–June 8); Committee on Conduct of the War established (December 20).

1862   Department of Agriculture established (May 15); Congress passes Homestead Act providing for citizens to acquire 160 acres of public land (May 20); Congress institutes income tax, approves land grants to build transcontinental railroad (July 1); Congress approves Morrill Act creating colleges funded by sales of public lands (July 2); Lincoln reads draft of Emancipation Proclamation to cabinet, accepts Seward's suggestion to defer issuance until after a Union victory (July 22); Lincoln responds to Greeley's open letter about emancipation (August 22); Union victory at Battle of Antietam halts Lee's invasion of the North (September 17); Lincoln issues preliminary Emancipation Proclamation (September 22).

1863   Emancipation Proclamation (January 1) grants freedom to slaves in rebelling states; Lincoln signs law creating first military draft (March 3); West Virginia admitted as a state (June 20); Union victories at Gettysburg (July 1–3) and Vicksburg (July 4) deal serious blows to Confederate hopes; antidraft riots in New York City (July 13–16).

1864   Grant given overall command of Union armies (March 10); William Tecumseh Sherman's army enters Atlanta (September 2); Nevada admitted as a state (October 31); Lincoln reelected over George B. McClellan (November 8).

1865   Davis and rest of Confederate government flee Richmond (April 2); Confederate surrender to Union forces at Appomattox Courthouse, effectively ending Civil War (April 9); Lincoln assassinated by John Wilkes Booth (April 14).

~NOTES~

Chapter 1. The Presidential Difference in the Civil War Era

1. Michael F. Holt, *The Political Crisis of the 1850s* (New York: Norton, 1978), 184. © 1978.

2. For reviews of the polls of experts and laypersons on the topic of presidential greatness, see Meena Bose, "Presidential Ratings: Lessons and Liabilities," in Meena Bose and Mark Landis, eds., *The Uses and Abuses of Presidential Ratings* (Hauppage, NY: Nova Science Publishers, 2003), 3–23; and Robert K. Murray and Tim H. Blessing, *Greatness in the White House: Rating the Presidents*, 2nd ed. (University Park: Pennsylvania State University Press, 1994).

3. Fred I. Greenstein, *The Presidential Difference: Leadership Style from FDR to Barack Obama*, 3rd ed. (Princeton, NJ: Princeton University Press, 2009) and *Inventing the Job of President: Leadership Style from George Washington to Andrew Jackson* (Princeton, NJ: Princeton University Press, 2009).

4. On the politics of admitting new states into the Union, see Russell D. Murphy, *Strategic Calculations and the Admission of New States into the Union, 1789–1960: Congress and the Politics of Statehood* (Lewiston, NY: Edwin Mellen Press, 2008).

5. *Congressional Globe*, 29th Cong., 2nd sess., p. 455; http://memory.loc.gov/cgi-bin/ampage?collId=llcg&fileName=018/llcg018.db&recNum=486.

6. From the "Appeal of the Independent Democrats," January 1854, quoted in Michael Holt, *The Fate of Their Country: Politicians, Slavery Extension, and the Coming of the Civil War* (New York: Hill and Wang, 2004), 141.

7. David Potter, "The Background of the Civil War," quoted in Thomas J. Pressly, ed., *Americans Interpret Their Civil War* (New York: Free Press, 1962), 10.

8. Allan Nevins, *Ordeal of the Union: Fruits of Manifest Destiny, 1847–1852*, vol. 1 (New York: Scribner's, 1947), ix.

9. William G. Andrews, "Presidential Conceptions of the Presidency," in Leonard W. Levy and Louis Fisher, eds., *Encyclopedia of the American Presidency*, vol. 3 (New York: Simon & Schuster, 1994), 1195.

Chapter 2. The Policy-Driven Political Style of James K. Polk

1. Quoted in Walter R. Borneman, *Polk: The Man Who Transformed the Presidency and America* (New York: Random House, 2008), 151. © 2008 Walter R. Borneman.

2. George Bancroft Papers, 1823–90, Manuscripts and Archives Division, New York Public Library, 1866.

3. Ralph Waldo Emerson, Journal entry, June ?, 1846, in Stephen E. Whicher, ed., *Selections from Ralph Waldo Emerson: An Organic Anthology* (Boston: Houghton Mifflin, 1960), 307. © 1957 Stephen E. Whicher.

4. George Bancroft Papers, 1823–90, Manuscripts and Archives Division, New York Public Library, 1866.

5. Charles Grier Sellers, *James K. Polk: Jacksonian, 1795–1843* (Princeton, NJ: Princeton University Press, 1957), 40.

6. John Reed Bumgarner, *Sarah Childress Polk: A Biography of the Remarkable First Lady* (Jefferson, NC: McFarland, 1997), 31, 85.

7. As Gary J. Kornblith has argued, if Clay had prevailed, it is unlikely that there would have been a Mexican War or a Mexican Cession. See Kornblith, "Rethinking the Coming of the Civil War: A Counterfactual Exercise," *Journal of American History* 90 (2003): 77.

8. All presidential statements quoted in this book are from the indispensable American Presidency Project based at the University of California–Santa Barbara unless otherwise indicated.

9. Norman A. Graebner, "James Polk," in Morton Borden, ed., *America's Ten Greatest Presidents* (Chicago: Rand McNally, 1961), 119–21.

10. Leonard D. White, *The Jacksonians: A Study in Administrative History, 1829–1861* (New York: Macmillan, 1954), 54.

11. Allan Nevins, *Polk: The Diary of a President—1845–1849, Covering the Mexican War, the Acquisition of Oregon, and the Conquest of California and the Southwest* (New York: Longmans Green, 1952), 138.

12. Nevins, *Polk: Diary,* 190. Despite Polk's claim to have no interest in extending the territory of slavery, it is instructive to note that he was a slave owner and actively engaged in buying and selling slaves even while in the White House—a fact he took pains to keep secret. For more on this subject, see William Dusinberre, *Slavemaster President: The Double Career of James Polk* (New York: Oxford University Press, 2007).

13. Graebner, "James Polk," 113–38.

14. Robert A. Dahl, *Who Governs? Democracy and Power in the American City* (New Haven, CT: Yale University Press, 1963), 309.

15. Sam W. Haynes, *James K. Polk and the Expansionist Impulse* (New York: Longman, 1997), 216.

16. David M. Pletcher, "James K. Polk," in Henry F. Graff, ed., *The Presidents: A Reference History*, 2nd ed. (New York: Scribner's, 1996), 170.

17. Nevins, *Polk: Diary*, 345.

18. Quoted in Nevins, *Polk: Diary*, xiv.

19. Sellers, *James K. Polk: Jacksonian*.

Chapter 3. The Rough and Ready Leadership of Zachary Taylor

1. This quote comes from David M. Potter, *The Impending Crisis: 1848–1861.* Completed and edited by Don E. Fehrenbacher (New York: Harper & Row, 1976), 96. © 1976 Estate of David M. Potter. Reprinted by permission of HarperCollins Publishers.

2. Quoted in David M. Potter, *The Impending Crisis: 1848–1861* (New York: Harper & Row, 1976), 87. © 1976 Estate of David M. Potter.

3. Zachary Taylor, Message to Congress, December 4, 1849, American Presidency Project, http://www.presidency.ucsb.edu/ws/index.php?pid=29490.

4. This chapter draws heavily on the wording, as well as the content, of John S. D. Eisenhower's *Zachary Taylor* (New York: Times Books, 2008). See also K. Jack Bauer, *Zachary Taylor: Soldier, Planter, Statesman of the Old Southwest* (Baton Rouge: Louisiana University Press, 1985); and Holman Hamilton, *Zachary Taylor: Soldier of the Republic* and *Zachary Taylor: Soldier in the White House* (Indianapolis, IN: Bobbs-Merrill, 1941 and 1951). For a recent study of the 1848 election, see Joel H. Silbey, *Party over Section: The Rough and Ready Presidential Election of 1848* (Lawrence: University Press of Kansas, 2009).

5. The declaration came in a letter that was meant to be made public; quoted at http://www.americanpresidents.org/letters/12.asp.

6. The critic was Ohio senator Thomas Corwin, who may have been influenced by his own unfulfilled presidential ambitions. Quoted in Glyndon G. Van Deusen, *The Jacksonian Era: 1828–1848* (New York: Harper & Row, 1963), 252.

7. Quoted in Bauer, *Zachary Taylor*, 232.

8. Quoted in Potter, *Impending Crisis*, 94.

9. Quoted in White House, Presidents, Zachary Taylor, http://www.whitehouse.gov/about/presidents/zacharytaylor.

10. Michael F. Holt, *The Fate of Their Country: Politicians, Slavery Extension, and the Coming of the Civil War* (New York: Hill and Wang, 2004), 77.

11. Potter, *Impending Crisis*, 97.

12. Bauer, *Zachary Taylor*, 262.

13. Quoted in Bauer, *Zachary Taylor*, 322.

14. Bauer, *Zachary Taylor*, 262.

15. Bauer, *Zachary Taylor*, 265.

16. Bauer, *Zachary Taylor*, xxiii.

17. Bauer, *Zachary Taylor*, 322.

Chapter 4. Millard Fillmore and the Compromise of 1850

1. Elbert B. Smith, "Millard Fillmore," in Leonard W. Levy and Louis Fisher, eds., *Encyclopedia of the American Presidency*, vol. 2 (New York: Simon & Schuster, 1994), 615.

2. Millard Fillmore, Special Message to Congress, August 6, 1850, American Presidency Project, http://www.presidency.ucsb.edu/ws/index.php?pid=68123&st=&st1=.

3. Millard Fillmore, First Annual Message to Congress, December 2, 1850, American Presidency Project, http://www.presidency.ucsb.edu/ws/index.php?pid=29491.

4. The standard biography of Fillmore is Robert J. Rayback, *Millard Fillmore: Biography of a President* (Buffalo, NY: Henry Stewart, 1959). For a recent work that departs from the typically positive treatment of Fillmore, see Paul Finkelman, *Millard Fillmore* (New York: Times Books, 2011).

5. Quoted in Michael F. Holt, "Millard Fillmore: 1850–1853," in Alan Brinkley and Davis Dyer, eds., *The Reader's Companion to the American Presidency* (Boston: Houghton Mifflin, 2000), 161.

6. David M. Potter, *The Impending Crisis: 1848 to 1861* (New York: Harper & Row, 1976), 107.

7. This section draws heavily on Holt, "Millard Fillmore."

8. Finkelman, *Fillmore*, 73–74.

9. On the Compromise of 1850, see Holman Hamilton, *Prologue to Conflict: The Crisis and Compromise of 1850* (Lexington: University Press of Kentucky, 2005), and Robert Remini, *At the Edge of the Precipice: Henry Clay and the Compromise That Saved the Union* (New York: Basic Books, 2010).

10. Quoted in Michael F. Holt, *The Fate of Their Country: Politicians, Slavery Extension, and the Coming of the Civil War* (New York: Hill and Wang, 2004), 82.

11. Quoted in Holt, *Fate of Their Country,* 84 (italics in original).

12. Quoted in Elbert B. Smith, *The Presidencies of Zachary Taylor & Millard Fillmore* (Lawrence: University Press of Kansas, 1988), 249.

13. Quoted in Philip B. Kunhardt Jr., Philip B. Kunhardt III, and Peter W. Kunhardt, *The American President* (New York: Riverhead Books, 1999), 221.

14. Potter, *Impending Crisis,* 110.

15. Quoted in Smith, *Presidencies of Taylor & Fillmore,* 261.

16. Daniel Walker Howe, *The Political Culture of the American Whigs* (Chicago: University of Chicago Press, 1984).

17. Rayback, *Millard Fillmore,* vii.

Chapter 5. Franklin Pierce and the Kansas-Nebraska Act

1. William W. Freehling, "Franklin Pierce," in Henry F. Graff, ed., *The Presidents: A Reference History*, 2nd ed. (New York: Charles Scribner's Sons, 1996), 189.

2. Franklin Pierce, Inaugural Address, March 4, 1853, American Presidency Project, http://www.presidency.ucsb.edu/ws/index.php?pid=25816.

3. Franklin Pierce, Inaugural Address, March 4, 1853.

4. For the rankings, see http://legacy.c-span.org/Presidential Survey/Overall-Ranking.aspx. On Pierce's historical reputation, see Meena Bose and Mark Landis, eds., *The Uses and Abuses of Presidential Ratings* (Hauppage, NY: Nova Science Publishers, 2003), 19. For works on the life and career of Franklin Pierce, see Michael F. Holt, *Franklin Pierce* (New York: Times Books, 2010); Peter A. Wallner, *Franklin Pierce: New Hampshire's Favorite Son* and *Franklin Pierce: Martyr for the Union* (Concord, NH: Plaidsweede, 2005 and 2009); and Larry Gara, *The Presidency of Franklin Pierce* (Lawrence: University Press of Kansas, 1991).

5. On Pierce's drinking, see Holt, *Franklin Pierce*, 7–8. On the alcoholic personality, see, for example, David S. Janowsky et al., "Underlying Personality Differences between Alcohol/Substance-Use Disorder Patients with and without an Affective Disorder," *Alcohol and Alcoholism* 34 (1999): 370–77.

6. For a comparison of the Pierces, see Holt, *Franklin Pierce*, 15–16. Examples of presidential spouses who performed this function include Dolley Madison, Eleanor Roosevelt, and Lady Bird Johnson.

7. William W. Freehling, "Franklin Pierce," in Henry F. Graff, ed., *The Presidents: A Reference History*, 2nd ed. (New York: Scribner's, 1996), 190.

8. Holt, *Franklin Pierce*, 43.

9. Quoted in Michael F. Holt, *The Fate of Their Country: Politicians, Slavery Extension, and the Coming of the Civil War* (New York: Hill and Wang, 2004), 90.

10. Quoted in James M. McPherson, ed., *"To the Best of My Ability": The American Presidents* (New York: Dorling Kindersley, 2001), 108.

11. From a document in the Nathaniel Hawthorne Collection in the George J. Mitchell Department of Special Collections & Archives at Bowdoin College, Brunswick, Maine.

12. See Freehling, "Franklin Pierce," 192–93, for a harsh view of Pierce's responsibility for the outcome of the Ostend meeting. Holt, *Franklin Pierce*, 63–65, is somewhat more forgiving of the president and places the memo, his response to it, and the reaction to the leak in a broader political context.

13. For a detailed account of the events described below, see David M. Potter, *The Impending Crisis: 1848–1861* (New York: Harper & Row, 1976), 145–76.

14. See Mel Laracey, *Presidents and the People: The Partisan Story of Going Public* (College Station: Texas A&M University Press, 2002), 95.

15. Freehling, "Franklin Pierce," 191.

16. See note 2.

Chapter 6. The Disastrous Presidency of James Buchanan

1. This quote comes from William E. Gienapp, "James Buchanan: 1857–1861," in Alan Brinkley and Davis Dyer, eds., *The Reader's Companion to the American Presidency* (Boston: Houghton Mifflin, 2000), 177. © 2000 Houghton Mifflin Harcourt Publishing Company. Used by permission of Houghton Mifflin Harcourt Publishing Company. All Rights Reserved.

2. James Buchanan, Inaugural Address, March 4, 1857, the American Presidency Project, http://www.presidency.ucsb.edu/ws/index.php?pid=25817.

3. James Buchanan, Fourth Annual Message to Congress, December 3, 1860, American Presidency Project, http://www.presidency.ucsb.edu/ws/index.php?pid=29501.

4. Biographies of Buchanan begin with the older George T. Curtis, *Life of James Buchanan, Fifteenth President of the United States* (New York: Harper and Brothers, 1883); and Philip S. Klein, *President James Buchanan* (University Park: Pennsylvania State University Press, 1962). Jean H. Baker's *James Buchanan* (New York: Times Books, 2004) is a provocative and important newer

study. Buchanan defended his actions in his memoir *Mr. Buchanan's Administration on the Eve of the Rebellion* (New York: D. Appleton, 1866; digital scanning by Digital Scanning Inc., Scituate, MA, 1999).

5. Quoted in James M. McPherson, *Battle Cry of Freedom: The Civil War Era* (New York: Ballantine Books, 1988), 177.

6. William E. Gienapp, "James Buchanan: 1857–1861," in Alan Brinkley and Davis Dyer, eds., *The Reader's Companion to the American Presidency* (Boston: Houghton Mifflin, 2000), 179.

7. Allan Nevins, *The Emergence of Lincoln*, vol. 1: *Douglas, Buchanan, and Party Chaos, 1857–1859* (New York: Scribner's, 1950), 400–403, effectively analyzes the election results.

8. James Buchanan, Fourth Annual Message to Congress, December 3, 1860, American Presidency Project, http://www.presidency.ucsb.edu/ws/index.php?pid=29501.

9. James Buchanan, Fourth Annual Message to Congress, December 3, 1860, American Presidency Project, http://www.presidency.ucsb.edu/ws/index.php?pid=29501.

10. Quoted in Jean H. Baker, *James Buchanan* (New York: Times Books, 2004), 68.

11. Quoted in Gienapp, "James Buchanan: 1857–1861," 177.

12. Jean Harvey Baker, "James Buchanan: 15th President, 1857–1861," in James M. McPherson, ed., *"To the Best of My Ability": The American Presidents* (New York: Dorling Kindersley, 2001), 110.

13. Quoted in Allen F. Cole, "Asserting His Authority: James Buchanan's Failed Vindication," *Journal of Pennsylvania History* 70 (2003): 93.

14. Mel Laracey, *Presidents and the People: The Partisan Story of Going Public* (College Station: Texas A&M University Press, 2002), 95–97.

15. Michael Birkner, introduction to *James Buchanan and the Political Crisis of the 1850s* (Selinsgrove, PA: Susquehanna University Press, 1996), 29.

16. Nevins, *Emergence of Lincoln*, 1:61.

17. Baker, *James Buchanan*, 148–49.

Chapter 7. Abraham Lincoln: Consummate Leader

1. Abraham Lincoln, Fragment on Slavery, circa July 1, 1854, in Roy B. Basler, ed., *The Collected Works of Abraham Lincoln*, vol. 2 (New Brunswick, NJ: Rutgers University Press, 1953), 222. This quotation is used with the permission of the Abraham Lincoln Association.

2. Abraham Lincoln, Letter to Brigadier General Don Carlos Buell, January 13, 1862, in Roy B. Basler, ed., *The Collected Works of Abraham Lincoln*, vol. 5 (New Brunswick, NJ: Rutgers University Press, 1953), 98. This quotation is used with the permission of the Abraham Lincoln Association.

3. Abraham Lincoln, Second Inaugural Address, March 4, 1865, American Presidency Project, http://www.presidency.ucsb.edu/ws/index.php?pid=25819.

4. The text refers to the C-SPAN poll of sixty-four presidential historians cited earlier (http://legacy.c-span.org/PresidentialSurvey/Overall-Ranking.aspx).

5. Lincoln ran for the state legislature the first two times with no party affiliation. Once in the state house, though, he gravitated to the Whigs, the party most consistent with his own upward social mobility. See Joel H. Silbey, "'Always a Whig in Politics': The Partisan Life of Abraham Lincoln," *Papers of the Abraham Lincoln Association* 8 (1986): 21–42. See also David Walker Howe, *The Political Culture of the American Whigs* (Chicago: University of Chicago Press, 1984).

6. James M. McPherson, "Abraham Lincoln," American National Biography Online, http://www.anb.org/articles/04/04-00631-article.html.

7. Joshua Wolf Shenk, *Lincoln's Melancholy: How Depression Challenged a President and Fueled His Greatness* (Boston: Houghton Mifflin, 2005), 116.

8. Don E. Fehrenbacher, ed., *Abraham Lincoln: Speeches and Writings, 1832–1858* (New York: Library of America, 1989), 315. See also Lewis E. Lehrman, *Lincoln at Peoria: The Turning Point* (Mechanicsburg, PA: Stackpole Books, 2008).

9. Harold Holzer, *Lincoln at Cooper Union: The Speech That Made Abraham Lincoln President* (New York: Simon & Schuster, 2004).

10. William Gienapp, "Abraham Lincoln and the Border States," *Journal of the Abraham Lincoln Association* 13 (1992): 13–46.

11. Ronald C. White Jr., *Lincoln's Greatest Speech: The Second Inaugural* (New York: Simon & Schuster, 2002).

12. On Lincoln's commitment to a nonpunitive policy to the former Confederates, see Ludwell H. Johnson, "Lincoln's Solution to the Problem of Peace Terms: 1864–1865," *Journal of Southern History* 34 (1968): 586.

13. Ronald C. White Jr., *A. Lincoln: A Biography* (New York: Random House, 2009), 393.

14. See, for example, William E. Gienapp, " 'No Bed of Roses': James Buchanan and Abraham Lincoln; Leadership in the Civil War Era," in Michael J. Birkner, ed., *James Buchanan and the Political Crisis of the 1850s* (Selinsgrove, PA: Susquehanna University Press, 1996), 118.

15. Michael Burlingame, *The Inner World of Abraham Lincoln* (Urbana: University of Illinois Press, 1994), 362. The earliest psychobiography of Lincoln was L. Pierce Clark, *Lincoln: A Psychobiography* (New York: Scribner's, 1933). More recent examples include George B. Forgie, *Patricide in the House Divided: A Psychological Interpretation of Lincoln and His Age* (New York: W. W. Norton, 1979), and Charles B. Strozier, *Lincoln's Quest for Union: Public and Private Meanings* (New York: Basic Books, 1982).

Chapter 8. What Difference Did the President Make?

1. Allan Nevins, *The Statesmanship of the Civil War* (New York: Collier Books, 1966), 30.

2. On the approaches these presidents employed to use the press to advance their purposes, see Mel Laracey, *Presidents and the People: The Partisan Story of Going Public* (College Station: Texas A&M University Press, 2002), 93–95, 115–16.

3. Tim De Mey and Eric Weber, "Explanation and Thought Experiments in History," *History and Theory* 42 (2003): 29. See also Giovanni Capoccia and R. Daniel Kelemen, "The Study of Critical Junctures: Theory, Narrative, and Counterfactuals in Historical Intuitionalism," *World Politics* 59 (2007): 1–26; Philip E.

Tetlock and Aaron Belkin, eds., *Counterfactual Thought Experiments in World Politics: Logical, Methodological, and Psychological Perspectives* (Princeton, NJ: Princeton University Press, 1996); and Fred I. Greenstein, *Personality and Politics: Problems of Evidence, Inference, and Conceptualization* (Chicago: Markham, 1969), chap. 2, and the writings there cited.

4. Holman Hamilton, *Prologue to Conflict: The Crisis and Compromise of 1850* (Lexington: University Press of Kentucky, 2005), 186.

5. Alan Brinkley and Davis Dyer, introduction to *The Reader's Companion to the American Presidency* (Boston: Houghton Mifflin, 2000), 5.

6. Angus Campbell, Philip E. Converse, Warren E. Miller, and Donald E. Stokes, *The American Voter* (New York: Wiley, 1960), 24–32; and Michael S. Lewis-Beck, William J. Jacoby, Helmut Northpoth, and Herbert E. Weisberg, *The American Voter Revisited* (Ann Arbor: University of Michigan Press, 2008), 22–28.

7. Lewis-Beck et al., *American Voter Revisited*, 22.

8. Thomas J. Pressly, *Americans Interpret Their Civil War* (New York: Free Press, 1962).

9. See, for example, Harold D. Lasswell and Abraham Kaplan, *Power and Society: A Framework for Political Inquiry* (New Haven, CT: Yale University Press, 1965), 3–4.

10. Malcolm Gladwell, *The Tipping Point: How Little Things Can Make a Big Difference* (Boston: Little, Brown, 2000).

11. For an inventory of such contingencies, see Greenstein, *Personality and Politics*, 40–61.

~ FURTHER READING ~

Chapter 1. The Presidential Difference in the Civil War Era

Meena Bose, "Presidential Ratings: Lessons and Liabilities," in Meena Bose and Mark Landis, eds., *The Uses and Abuses of Presidential Ratings* (Hauppage, NY: Nova Science Publishers, 2003), 3–23; and Robert K. Murray and Tim H. Blessing, *Greatness in the White House: Rating the Presidents*, 2nd ed. (University Park: Pennsylvania State University Press, 1994). For the background of the period, see such works as Michael Holt, *The Fate of Their Country: Politicians, Slavery Extension, and the Coming of the Civil War* (New York: Hill and Wang, 2004); Russell D. Murphy, *Strategic Calculations and the Admission of New States into the Union, 1789–1960: Congress and the Politics of Statehood* (Lewiston, NY: Edwin Mellen Press, 2008); and Allan Nevins, *Ordeal of the Union: Fruits of Manifest Destiny, 1847–1852*, vol. 1 (New York: Scribner's, 1947). For a useful collection of essays on causes of the Civil War, see Thomas J. Pressly, ed., *Americans Interpret Their Civil War* (New York: Free Press, 1962).

Chapter 2. The Policy-Driven Political Style of James K. Polk

There has been no shortage of biographies of Polk and studies of his presidency. See Paul H. Bergeron, *The Presidency of James K. Polk* (Lawrence: University Press of Kansas, 1987); Walter R. Borneman, *Polk: The Man Who Transformed the Presidency and America* (New York: Random House, 2008); Sam W. Haynes, *James K. Polk and the Expansionist Impulse*, 3rd ed. (New York: Longman, 2006); Thomas M. Leonard, *James K. Polk: A Clear and Unquestionable Destiny* (Wilmington, DE: Scholarly Resources Book, 2001); Eugene Irving McCormac, *James K. Polk: A Political Biography* (Berkeley: University of California Press, 1922); Charles Allan McCoy, *Polk and the Presidency* (Austin: University of Texas Press, 1960); Robert W. Merry, *A Country of Vast Designs: James K. Polk, the Mexican War, and the Conquest of the American Continent* (New York: Simon & Schuster, 2009); John Seigenthaler, *James K. Polk* (New York: Times Books, 2003); Charles Grier Sellers, *James K. Polk: Jacksonian, 1795–1843* (Princeton, NJ: Princeton University Press, 1957); and Sellers, *James K. Polk: Continentalist, 1843–1846* (Princeton, NJ: Princeton University Press, 1966). John Reed Bumgarner provides a useful biography of the First Lady: *Sarah Childress Polk: A Biography of the Remarkable First Lady* (Jefferson, NC: McFarland, 1997)

For valuable short overviews of Polk's life and presidency, see Norman A. Graebner, "James Polk," in Morton Borden, ed., *American's Ten Greatest Presidents* (Chicago: Rand McNally, 1961), 113–38; Michael W. Holt, "James K. Polk," in Alan Brinkley and Davis Dyer, eds., *The Reader's Companion to the American Presidency* (Boston: Houghton Mifflin, 2000), 141–50; and David M. Pletcher, "James K. Polk," in Henry F. Graff, ed., *The Presidents: A Reference History*, 2nd ed. (New York: Scribner's, 1996), 155–73. Polk kept a detailed diary that has been an invaluable source for scholars. It exists in a four-volume edition (James K. Polk, *The Diary of James K. Polk during His Presidency*, ed. Milo Milton Quaife [Chicago: A. C. McClurg, 1910]) and a one-volume abridgment edited by Allan Nevins (*Polk: The Diary of a President—1845–1849, Covering the Mexican War, the Acquisition of Oregon, and the Conquest of California and the Southwest* [New York: Longmans Green, 1929]). See also Leonard D. White, *The Jacksonians: A Study in Administrative History, 1829–1861* (New York: Macmillan, 1954).

Chapter 3. The Rough and Ready Leadership of Zachary Taylor

Biographies include Jack K. Bauer, *Zachary Taylor: Soldier, Planter, Statesman of the Old Southwest* (Baton Rouge: Louisiana State University Press, 1993); John

S. D. Eisenhower's *Zachary Taylor* (New York: Times Books, 2008); Holman Hamilton, *Zachary Taylor: Soldier of the Republic* (Indianapolis, IN: Bobbs-Merrill, 1941); Holman Hamilton, *Zachary Taylor: Soldier in the White House* (Indianapolis, IN: Bobbs-Merrill, 1951).

Useful studies of the background to the period and of Taylor's presidency include Holman Hamilton, *Prologue to Conflict: The Crisis and Compromise of 1850* (Lexington: University Press of Kentucky, 1964; reprinted with an introduction by Michael F. Holt, 2005); Michael F. Holt, *The Political Crisis of the 1850s* (New York: Norton, 1978); Michael F. Holt, *The Rise and Fall of the American Whig Party: Jacksonian Politics and the Onset of the Civil War* (New York: Oxford University Press, 1999); Daniel Walker Howe, *The Political Culture of the American Whigs* (Chicago: University of Chicago Press, 1984); James M. McPherson, *Battle Cry of Freedom: The Civil War Era* (New York: Oxford University Press, 1988); Robert Remini, *At the Edge of the Precipice: Henry Clay and the Compromise That Saved the Union* (New York: Basic Books, 2010); Joel H. Silbey, *Party over Section: The Rough and Ready Presidential Election of 1848* (Lawrence: University Press of Kansas, 2009); and Elbert B. Smith, *The Presidencies of Zachary Taylor & Millard Fillmore* (Lawrence: University Press of Kansas, 1988).

Chapter 4. Millard Fillmore and the Compromise of 1850

Robert J. Rayback, *Millard Fillmore: Biography of a President* (Buffalo, NY: Henry Stewart, 1959), which suffers from its author's lack of access to the papers at Oswego, which were discovered in the 1970s. For a briefer biography, see Michael F. Holt, "Millard Fillmore: 1850–1853," in Alan Brinkley and Davis Dyer, eds., *The Reader's Companion to the American Presidency* (Boston: Houghton Mifflin, 2000).

On the period and the issues, see also Elbert B. Smith, *The Presidencies of Zachary Taylor & Millard Fillmore* (Lawrence: University Press of Kansas, 1988), which is the only work that takes the position that the replacement of Taylor by Fillmore was necessary for the passage of the Compromise of 1850. On the feud between Fillmore and Seward, which played such an important part in shaping Fillmore's career, see Harry J. Carman and Reinhard H. Luthin, "The Seward-Fillmore Feud and the Crisis of 1850" and "The Seward-Fillmore Feud and the Disruption of the Whig Party," *New York History* 24 (1943): 163–84, 335–57. On Fillmore's role in the Compromise of 1850, see Holman Hamilton, *Prologue to Conflict: The Crisis and Compromise of 1850* (Lexington: University Press of Kentucky, 1964; reprinted with an introduction by Michael F. Holt, 2005), and Robert Remini, *At the Edge of the Precipice: Henry Clay and the Compromise That Saved the Union* (New York: Basic Books, 2010). For more on the Whig Party, see Daniel Walker Howe, *The Political Culture of the American Whigs* (Chicago: University of Chicago Press, 1984).

Chapter 5. Franklin Pierce and the Kansas-Nebraska Act

The literature on Franklin Pierce is not large. Nathaniel Hawthorne, *Life of Franklin Pierce* (Boston: Ticknor, Reed, and Fields, 1852) was Pierce's campaign biography. Hawthorne was a college friend. For many years, the most comprehensive biography of Pierce was Roy Nichols, *Franklin Pierce: Young Hickory of the Granite Hill*, 2nd ed. rev. (Philadelphia: University of Pennsylvania Press, 1958). There is now a more comprehensive two-volume biography by Peter A. Wallner, *Franklin Pierce: New Hampshire's Favorite Son* (Concord, NH: Plaidswede, 2004) and *Franklin Pierce: Martyr for the Union* (Concord, NH: Plaidswede, 2007). For an excellent short work, see Michael F. Holt, *Franklin Pierce* (New York: Times Books, 2010). A shorter biography and assessment can be found in William W. Freehling, "Franklin Pierce," in Henry F. Graff, ed., *The Presidents: A Reference History*, 2nd ed. (New York: Scribner's, 1996).

The standard work on the Pierce presidency is Larry Gara, *The Presidency of Franklin Pierce* (Lawrence: University Press of Kansas, 1991). Other works on the period that are useful include Michael F. Holt, *The Fate of Their Country: Politicians, Slavery Extension, and the Coming of the Civil War* (New York: Hill and Wang, 2004); and David M. Potter, *The Impending Crisis: 1848–1861* (New York: Harper & Row, 1976).

Chapter 6. The Disastrous Presidency of James Buchanan

John B. Moore, ed., *The Works of James Buchanan*, 12 vols. (repr., New York: Antiquarian Press, 1960), is a comprehensive primary source on Buchanan. Biographies of the Pennsylvania president include Philip S. Klein, *President James Buchanan* (University Park: Pennsylvania State University Press, 1962); and George T. Curtis, *Life of James Buchanan, Fifteenth President of the United States* (New York: Harper and Brothers, 1883). Buchanan's own defense of his presidency is the impersonally titled *Mr. Buchanan's Administration on the Eve of the Rebellion* (New York: D. Appleton, 1866; digital scanning by Digital Scanning Inc., Scituate, MA, 1999). A discussion of the response to that work can be found in Allen F. Cole, "Asserting His Authority: James Buchanan's Failed Vindication," *Journal of*

Pennsylvania History 70 (2003): 81–97. For a provocative more recent work, see Jean H. Baker, *James Buchanan* (New York: Times Books, 2004). A brief biography is William E. Gienapp, "James Buchanan: 1857–1861," in Alan Brinkley and Davis Dyer, eds., *The Reader's Companion to the American Presidency* (Boston: Houghton Mifflin, 2000).

Also see Philip Auchampaugh, *James Buchanan and His Cabinet on the Eve of Secession* (Lancaster, PA, privately printed, 1926; repr., Boston: J. S. Canner, 1965), and the valuable compilation Michael Birkner, ed., *James Buchanan and the Political Crisis of the 1850's* (Selinsgrove, PA: Susquehanna Press, 1996). On the Buchanan presidency, see Elbert B. Smith, *The Presidency of James Buchanan* (Lawrence: University Press of Kansas, 1975). For background on the period, see James M. McPherson, *Battle Cry of Freedom: The Civil War Era* (New York: Ballantine Books, 1988); and Allan Nevins, *The Emergence of Lincoln*, vol. 1: *Douglas, Buchanan, and Party Chaos, 1857–1859* (New York, Scribner's, 1950).

Chapter 7. Abraham Lincoln: Consummate Leader

Lincoln's writings can be found in *The Collected Works of Abraham Lincoln*, ed. Roy P. Basler (8 vols. and an index) (New Brunswick, NJ: Rutgers University Press,

1953–55), with the addition of *The Collected Works of Abraham Lincoln: Supplement, 1832–1865*, ed. Roy P. Basler (New Brunswick, NJ: Rutgers University Press, 1974). The most important of Lincoln's letters and other writings have been selected by Don E. Fehrenbacher and published in two volumes entitled *Abraham Lincoln: Speeches and Writings, 1832–1858* (New York: Library of America, 1989).

The major one-volume biography of Lincoln is David Herbert Donald, *Lincoln* (New York: Simon & Schuster, 1995). For an outstanding brief biography, see William E. Gienapp, *Abraham Lincoln and Civil War America: A Biography* (New York: Oxford University Press, 2002). The most detailed modern biography is Michael Burlingame's two-volume *Abraham Lincoln: A Life* (Baltimore: John Hopkins University Press, 2008), which consumes almost 2,000 pages. See also Mark E. Neel, *The Abraham Lincoln Encyclopedia* (New York: McGraw-Hill, 1981).

Studies of particular aspects of Lincoln's life and presidency include Gabor Boritt, *Lincoln and the Economics of the American Dream* (Memphis: Memphis State University Press, 1978); G. S. Boritt and N. O. Forness, *The Historians' Lincoln* (Urbana: University of Illinois Press, 1988); Michael Burlingame, *The Inner World of Abraham Lincoln* (Urbana: University of Illinois Press, 1994); David Donald, *Lincoln Reconsid-*

ered: *Essays on the Civil War Era*, 2nd ed. (New York: Vintage Books, 1961); and Joshua Wolf Shenk, *Lincoln's Melancholy: How Depression Challenged a President and Fueled His Greatness* (Boston: Houghton Mifflin, 2005). A valuable work on Lincoln and his political context is Allan Nevins, *The Emergence of Lincoln*, 2 vols. (New York: Charles Scribner's Sons, 1950). Also see Don E. Fehrenbacher, *Lincoln in Text and Context: Collected Essays* (Stanford, CA: Stanford University Press, 1987) and *Prelude to Greatness: Lincoln in the 1850's* (Stanford, CA: Stanford University Press, 1962); James M. McPherson, *Abraham Lincoln and the Second American Revolution* (New York: Oxford University Press, 1990); Lewis E. Lehrman, *Lincoln at Peoria: The Turning Point* (Mechanicsburg, PA: Stackpole Books, 2008); and Phillip Shaw Paludan, *The Presidency of Abraham Lincoln* (Lawrence: University Press of Kansas, 1994).

Chapter 8. What Difference Did the President Make?

On counterfactuals, see Tim De Mey and Eric Weber, "Explanation and Thought Experiments in History," *History and Theory* 42 (2003): 28–38; Giovanni Capoccia and R. Daniel Kelemen, "The Study of Critical Junctures: Theory, Narrative, and Counterfactuals in Historical Intuitionalism," *World Politics* 59 (2007):

1–26; Philip E. Tetlock and Aaron Belkin, eds., *Counterfactual Thought Experiments in World Politics: Logical, Methodological, and Psychological Perspectives* (Princeton, NJ: Princeton University Press, 1996); and Fred I. Greenstein, *Personality and Politics: Problems of Evidence, Inference, and Conceptualization* (Chicago: Markham, 1969), chap. 2, and the writings there cited. The funnel of causality is explored in Michael S. Lewis-Beck, William J. Jacoby, Helmut Northpoth, and Herbert E. Weisberg, *The American Voter Revisited* (Ann Arbor: University of Michigan Press, 2008), 22–28, while Malcolm Gladwell looks at tipping points in *The Tipping Point: How Little Things Can Make a Big Difference* (Boston: Little, Brown, 2000).

~ ACKNOWLEDGMENTS ~

I am indebted to a number of students of the Civil War era for comments on portions of this manuscript, including Jean H. Baker, Michael J. Birkner, Allen C. Guelzo, James M. McPherson, and two anonymous reviewers for Princeton University Press. I also profited from the feedback of audiences at Princeton University and the universities of Essex, Oxford, Leeds, and London.

This project has been supported by fellowship for emeritus faculty awarded to me by the Mellon Foundation. That in turn has enabled me to employ two able editors—Linda Benson and Dale Anderson. Finally, Chuck Myers of Princeton University has been a continuing source of advice and encouragement.

I would like to thank Michael Holt for permission to include an excerpt from *The Fate of Their Country: Politicians, Slavery Extension, and the Coming of the Civil War* (New York: Hill and Wang, 2004, p. 5 © 2004) as the epigraph to this book.

~INDEX~

Note: References to figures conform to the following pattern: 99f. refers to the figure which is found on page 99.